"With grace, patience, pastoral tenderness, and honesty, Wayne Grudem takes a careful look at biblical teaching on the gospel and evangelism as he critically examines the teaching of what is called Free Grace. As well intentioned as this position is, Grudem argues it falls short in five areas. He is fair, citing Free Grace materials in full and engaging biblical texts with care. I commend this book as one who has had similar discussions on these topics with people who hold this position, people whom I also respect as Grudem does."

Darrell L. Bock, Executive Director of Cultural Engagement, Howard G. Hendricks Center; Senior Research Professor of New Testament Studies, Dallas Theological Seminary

"Within evangelicalism, there is a kind of presentation of the Bible's teaching on grace that actually diminishes what the Bible teaches about grace, while purporting to elaborate and emphasize it. Wayne Grudem carefully, charitably, wisely, and pastorally takes on that kind of teaching in this book. This is an issue that especially pastors and those preparing to be pastors need to think through clearly, because confusion in our teaching and preaching on this will harm the sheep and our witness."

J. Ligon Duncan III, Chancellor and CEO, Reformed Theological Seminary, Jackson

"Ever so fair and irenic, New Testament scholar and trusted theologian Wayne Grudem gives no quarter to the purveyors of the so-called Free Grace gospel as he exposes their troubling pattern of selective reading of the standard Greek lexicons, as well as of famed theologians, to effect the illusion of support for their position. Grudem does more than demolish a house of cards as he pastorally lays out what the New Testament says about the nature of the gospel, repentance, faith, and assurance. Grudem's critique is a gift of love to the church universal, and especially to those under the unfortunate thrall of errant teaching."

R. Kent Hughes, Visiting Professor of Practical Theology, Westminster Theological Seminary

"The so-called 'lordship controversy' has been simmering for several decades now. I'm thankful for several fresh resources that deal with these matters accurately and succinctly. Wayne Grudem's book in particular is an excellent and very useful digest of the main doctrinal and biblical issues under debate. He answers the questions with uncommon clarity and skill, always from Scripture."

John MacArthur, Pastor, Grace Community Church, Sun Valley, California; President, The Master's College and Seminary

"Credence without commitment and assurance without action are the hall-marks of the so-called Free Grace version of the gospel of Jesus Christ. It is, however, unbiblical, anti-evangelical, and sub-Christian, as Grudem's patient and well-informed analysis clearly shows."

J. I. Packer, Board of Governors' Professor of Theology, Regent College

"Wayne Grudem's book on Free Grace is the best I have read on the subject, and I commend it with enthusiasm for several reasons. First, it is biblically saturated, showing us again and again what the Scriptures say. Second, Grudem's explanations are so clear that virtually any Christian can read and understand this book. Third, the book is amazingly kind, generous, and charitable. Grudem isn't on the attack. He loves those with whom he disagrees, and that love shines through the book. Fourth, Grudem recognizes the issue is massively important since it has to do with the nature of the gospel we preach and proclaim. He argues convincingly that works are a necessary fruit of salvation, which doesn't threaten free grace but upholds what the great Reformers taught about salvation."

Thomas R. Schreiner, James Buchanan Harrison Professor of New Testament Interpretation and Associate Dean of the School of Theology, The Southern Baptist Theological Seminary

"This excellent and insightful book is much needed in the church today, especially in view of ever-increasing focus on the nature of the gospel. His analysis of the ill-named Free Grace movement is clear, thoroughly biblical, and entirely persuasive. He deals forthrightly yet charitably with the views of those who advocate this mistaken conception of the gospel of God's grace in Jesus Christ. All Christians will benefit greatly from reading Grudem's analysis. I cannot recommend this book too highly."

Sam Storms, Lead Pastor for Preaching and Vision, Bridgeway Church, Oklahoma City, Oklahoma

"This book is charitable yet rock-solid in its penetrating insights regarding the Free Grace movement. The soteriology of this movement is thoroughly consistent—and deeply flawed. Grudem has addressed a number of the key issues and texts in a gracious and gentle manner. I recommend it to anyone who is interested in the Free Grace movement and its implications for the gospel."

Daniel B. Wallace, Senior Professor of New Testament Studies, Dallas Theological Seminary

"With care and weighty biblical and historical argumentation, Grudem applies his clear-headed reasoning to show where the Free Grace view has gone wrong. Because this disagreement has to do with the very nature of the gospel, saving faith, and the basis of assurance, it is critical that Christians understand rightly what Scripture teaches on these matters. *"Free Grace" Theology* provides an excellent guide to understanding why the traditional Protestant and Reformed view of these matters accurately expresses biblical teaching and where the Free Grace view misleads. Every Christian can benefit from reading this book, to grow in clarity and conviction of understanding of what salvation by faith alone truly means."

Bruce A. Ware, T. Rupert and Lucille Coleman Professor of Christian Theology, The Southern Baptist Theological Seminary

Not correct

"Free Grace" Theology

5 Ways It Diminishes the Gospel

Wayne Grudem

CROSSWAY
WHEATON, ILLINOIS

Trade paperback ISBN: 978-1-4335-5114-7
ePub ISBN: 978-1-4335-5117-8
PDF ISBN: 978-1-4335-5115-4
Mobipocket ISBN: 978-1-4335-5116-1

Library of Congress Cataloging-in-Publication Data

Names: Grudem, Wayne A., author.
Title: Free grace theology : 5 ways it diminishes the gospel / Wayne A. Grudem.
Description: Wheaton : Crossway, 2016. | Includes bibliographical references and index.
Identifiers: LCCN 2015047231 (print) | LCCN 2016012961 (ebook) | ISBN 9781433551147 (pb) | ISBN 9781433551178 (epub) | ISBN 9781433551154 (pdf) | ISBN 9781433551161 (mobi)
Subjects: LCSH: Grace (Theology) | Salvation—Christianity.
Classification: LCC BT761.3 .G78 2016 (print) | LCC BT761.3 (ebook) | DDC 234—dc23
LC record available at http://lccn.loc.gov/2015047231

Crossway is a publishing ministry of Good News Publishers.

BP   26   25   24   23   22   21   20   19   18   17   16
15   14   13   12   11   10   9   8   7   6   5   4   3   2   1

To
Darryl DelHousaye,
president of Phoenix Seminary,
supporter and advocate for all his faculty members,
tireless promoter of everything that advances
the work of God's kindom,
my pastor for many years,
and my friend.

Therefore, my beloved brothers, be steadfast, immovable,
always abounding in the work of the Lord,
knowing that in the Lord your labor is not in vain.
(1 Cor. 15:58)

Contents

Acknowledgments

Many people helped me in the production of this book, and I want to express my appreciation here.

I particularly wish to thank Roger Fankhauser, president of the Free Grace Alliance, and others working with him, who sent me a detailed, courteous, and thoughtful interaction with an oral presentation that I made on this topic in March 2014 at Scottsdale Bible Church. They did not persuade me with their arguments, but I hope that their correspondence has made my representation of their position more precise.

In addition, I wish to express much appreciation to Fred Chay, for thirteen years a colleague of mine at Phoenix Seminary, for his patience with me in numerous extended discussions on these matters. Fred is a highly skilled, articulate, and thoughtful theologian, and though in the end we did not agree on the issues discussed in this book, we agreed on many, many other things, and I believe that we continue to count each other as valued friends and colleagues in the work of the kingdom of God. My excellent teaching assistant Jeff Phillips also helped to sharpen my thinking on these issues.

Others who do not hold a Free Grace position also helped me to clarify my thinking and to understand the Free Grace position better, including my president, Darryl DelHousaye; and my academic dean, Bing Hunter, at Phoenix Seminary; pastor Jamie Rasmussen at Scottsdale Bible Church; pastor Josh Vincent at Trinity Bible Church; and my teaching assistants John Paul Stepanian, Daniel Malakowsky, Jason Miller, and Joshua McCoy; as well as good friends Steve and Kitty Oman. Jenny Miller helped me at several points with typing and details of manuscript preparation. Librarians Doug Olbert and Mitch Miller helped me with finding resources in the library, and Don Baltzer helped with modifying the depiction of my seminary key ring (see p. 37). Greg Salazar helped me with some research at the Cambridge University Library, and Alice Jackson provided timely help in manuscript printing at the Tyndale House Library. Trent Poling rescued me from a near disaster when, nearing the end of my work, I accidentally gave Microsoft Word a command to "sort" all the paragraphs in the book alphabetically! My friend Dan Wallace gave me many helpful suggestions on an earlier form of this manuscript, and Mark Chapman provided me with historical materials on different views of the nature of conversion. Joshua McCoy compiled the bibliography and helped with proofreading. Jason Miller helped me solve several computer problems.

But my greatest help has come from my wife, Margaret, who continues to encourage me in my writing as she has done with many other books, delightfully caring for our home and nourishing me with wonderful meals as I write, cheering me up, praying for me, and supporting this writing ministry in so many ways.

Finally, I want to give the most thanks of all to my Lord and

Savior Jesus Christ, who (I believe) guided me to work on this project in spite of my resistance to the idea for several years and gave me strength to complete the project. I pray that he will continue to guide this book into the right hands and make it persuasive to others, but only to the extent that he deems it faithful to his Word, the Bible.

Wayne Grudem
June 2015

Introduction

It is with some reluctance that I write this book. Many of the people who hold the Free Grace viewpoint that I disagree with in the pages that follow have been my friends for years, even decades. They strongly affirm the complete inerrancy of the Bible, the Trinity, the full deity of Christ, the substitutionary atonement of Christ for our sins, and dozens upon dozens of other important doctrinal convictions. Many of them lead exemplary Christian lives. They are genuine brothers and sisters in Christ, and I appreciate their friendship and their partnership in the work of God's kingdom here on earth. Therefore I consider this book to be part of a serious, earnest discussion of a significant difference, but a difference that is still among friends.

Yet this book is about more than the Free Grace controversy. It is about the nature of the gospel that we proclaim in evangelism. The New Testament repeatedly emphasizes the need for repentance from sin (in the sense of an internal resolve to turn from sin) as a crucial part of genuine saving faith. As I worked on this book, I became increasingly concerned that much of modern evangelicalism has a tendency to avoid or water down any call for unbelievers to sincerely repent of their sins (not merely to "change their minds") as part of coming to trust in Christ for forgiveness of those sins (see chapter 2).

This book also deals with assurance of salvation. How can I know if I'm really a born-again Christian, and how can I know that I will be saved for eternity? I'm concerned that there is considerable uncertainty about assurance in the evangelical world today, and therefore I have attempted to explain the New Testament material on assurance and also to treat sensitively the question of pastoral care for those who are wondering if they are truly saved (see chapter 3).

Finally, this book deals with the nature of saving faith in the New Testament, explaining that it is a fuller and richer concept than merely believing that what the Bible says is factually and historically true (though that is important). Saving faith involves coming into a personal relationship with Jesus Christ, coming into his presence and deciding to place my trust in him as a living, divine person who sees and hears us every moment and who knows the deepest thoughts of my heart. I am concerned that this emphasis on placing our trust in the *person* of Christ is too often missing in our evangelism today (see chapter 4).

What I have found to be true in many previous theological disputes has also proven to be true in the dispute before us here: the Lord has several purposes in allowing a doctrinal controversy into his church. In particular, I suspect that the Lord would have us not only disagree graciously with those who hold the Free Grace position but also think carefully about our own understanding and practice regarding the nature of the gospel, repentance, saving faith, and assurance of salvation.

Many evangelicals today who have never heard of the Free Grace movement have unknowingly moved too far in the direction of Free Grace teaching anyway. They have become too timid about urging unbelievers to repent of their sins as they come to trust in Christ (in part because we live in a culture that would condemn any call for repentance as legalistic and judgmental), too vague about explaining what it is to trust in Christ personally, and too uncertain about how and when to give assurance of salvation to those who are part of our churches.

For all these reasons, I hope that this book will be useful for evangelical Christians today.

A. What is the Free Grace gospel?

The Free Grace position claims that we are justified *by faith alone*.[1] I have no disagreement with that statement in itself—in fact, justification by faith alone has been a primary belief of Protestants since the time of Martin Luther and the Protestant Reformation.[2]

The problem comes when the Free Grace movement understands "alone," in the phrase "justified by faith alone," in a novel way. Protestants generally have taken "alone" to mean that nothing else *helps* or nothing else *contributes* in our

---

[1] For example, the "Covenant" that defines the doctrinal position of the Free Grace Alliance says, "The Grace of God in justification is an unconditional free gift," and, "The sole means of receiving the free gift of eternal life is faith in the Lord Jesus Christ, the Son of God, whose substitutionary death on the cross fully satisfied the requirement for our justification." Accessed January 19, 2015, http://www.freegracealliance.com/covenant.htm.
[2] See discussion below for evidence from many Protestant leaders. The phrase "justification by faith alone" captures the important disagreement between Protestants and Roman Catholics, who believe that we are justified by faith plus our use of the means of grace. In Protestant theology, *justification* is defined as follows: "Justification is an instantaneous legal act of God in which he (1) thinks of our sins as forgiven and Christ's righteousness as belonging to us, and (2) declares us to be righteous in his sight." Wayne Grudem, *Systematic Theology* (Grand Rapids, MI: Zondervan, 1994), 723.

obtaining justification from God. Our faith is the only thing that God requires of us—not good works, not offering some sacrifice, not performing some ritual or ceremony, not the use of some means of grace—just faith alone.

But Free Grace proponents have gone beyond the claim that God asks of us nothing more than faith when he justifies us. They have made an additional claim: that faith *occurs by itself* when a person is justified, in the sense that no other human actions necessarily accompany faith (such as repentance from sin or doing good works after we are justified).[3]

Then, because they argue that "nothing else must necessarily be present" with faith, the Free Grace movement teaches that it is wrong to say that:

repentance from sin must accompany faith

or

any other human activities necessarily result from faith, such as *good works* or continuing to believe.[4]

This Free Grace understanding of "justification by faith alone" leads to several significant pastoral practices, such as

---

[3] Free Grace advocates certainly *encourage* good works as the "normal" and "expected" response to God's saving grace, but they insist that no evident works must necessarily result from saving faith.

[4] For example, the Covenant of the Free Grace Alliance says, "The Gospel of Grace should always be presented with such clarity and simplicity that no impression is left that justification requires any step, response, or action in addition to faith in the Lord Jesus Christ." Their literature then argues that repentance from sin is not a necessary part of saving faith (most of them define *repentance* as just a "change of mind" and not an inner resolve to turn from sin). They also argue that good works should not be said to necessarily follow from saving faith. (I provide documentation of these points from Free Grace authors in the following pages.)

In evangelism. Evangelistic messages generally should not include any call to repentance, in the sense of an inward resolve to turn away from sin (this is said to be adding "works" to faith).

In giving assurance to people who deny their faith. People who accurately understood the gospel and sincerely said that they believed in Christ at some time in the past but now say that they no longer believe in Christ are likely to be still saved, and we can assure them that they are saved (because justifying faith is a one-time act).

In giving warnings to people who persist in sinful conduct. A professing Christian's sinful conduct should not ordinarily be used as a basis for warning the person that he or she might not be saved (rather, we should say that the person is foolishly not living according to who he or she really is).

In giving assurance to people who continue to produce good works. A professing Christian's righteous and godly conduct of life ("good works") should not ordinarily be used as one basis for giving that person assurance of salvation.

Where did the modern Free Grace movement come from? As far as I can tell, it stems primarily from a minority view among the faculty members at Dallas Theological Seminary. More particularly, it stems from an aggressive promotion of the Free Grace viewpoint by Zane Hodges (1932–2008), who taught New Testament at Dallas Theological Seminary for twenty-seven years, from 1959 to 1986.

But that recent origin does not mean that the movement

is insignificant. Although only a minority of Dallas Seminary professors held a Free Grace view, Zane Hodges was an exceptionally persuasive teacher, and every year some students adopted his view. Then, through these students, the Free Grace movement gained a remarkable worldwide influence, especially in discouraging Christians from including any explicit call to repentance in their presentations of the gospel. (I have been surprised how many Christian leaders in various parts of the world have said to me, "I'm glad you're writing about this.")

B. Why I do not use the term *Lordship Salvation.*

Some readers may wonder why I do not use the term *Lordship Salvation* in discussing this topic. In fact, the matters that I discuss here have in previous years often been referred to as the "Lordship Salvation controversy."[5] But as I researched this topic, it became increasingly apparent that the phrase *Lordship Salvation* was a decidedly misleading and unfortunate summary of the central issues involved.[6] In brief, popular terms, the controversy was sometimes summarized as follows.

---

[5] E.g., note the titles of these books: Zane Hodges, *Absolutely Free! A Biblical Reply to Lordship Salvation* (Grand Rapids, MI: Zondervan, 1989); Kenneth Gentry, *Lord of the Saved: Getting to the Heart of the Lordship Debate* (Phillipsburg, NJ: P&R, 1992; repr. Fountain Inn, SC: Victorious House, 2001); Michael Horton, ed., *Christ the Lord: The Reformation and Lordship Salvation* (Grand Rapids, MI: Baker, 1992; repr. Eugene, OR: Wipf & Stock, 2008); Charles Bing, *Lordship Salvation: A Biblical Evaluation and Response* (Maitland, FL: Xulon Press, 2010).

[6] I was glad to see that John MacArthur Jr. said bluntly, "I don't like the term *lordship salvation.* I reject the connotation intended by those who coined the phrase. It insinuates that a submissive heart is extraneous or supplementary to saving faith. Although I have reluctantly used the term to describe my views, it is a concession to popular usage." John F. MacArthur Jr., *Faith Works: The Gospel According to the Apostles* (Dallas: Word, 1993), 23. The habit of referring to this as the "Lordship Salvation controversy" probably stems from a two-part article in the once-popular magazine *Eternity* 10.9 (September 1959), "Must Christ Be Lord to Be Savior? No . . . Yes," 13–18, 36, 48, with Everett Harrison arguing the *no* viewpoint and John Stott arguing the *yes* viewpoint on the opposite pages. Although the title of that article pointed to some differences between the two authors, it did so in an imprecise and confusing way, for Stott never claims that *perfect* submission to

1) Some people believe that you can accept Jesus *as Savior but not as Lord* (the Free Grace position).

2) Other people believe that you have to accept Jesus *as both Savior and Lord* (those who do not hold the Free Grace position but rather what was termed the "Lordship Salvation" position)

The problem is that neither side will ever win or lose the argument when it is framed in those terms. The Free Grace supporters who hold the first position still affirm strongly that Jesus is in fact Lord over the entire universe and over all of our lives, even though we imperfectly submit to his lordship.[7] And those on the non-Free Grace side, those who hold the second position, all agree that our submission to Christ's lordship is imperfect in this life.[8]

So both sides agree that Jesus is Lord of our lives in some sense and is not fully Lord of our lives in another sense. Trying to define precisely *how much* Jesus has to be acknowledged as Lord for genuine saving faith becomes an increasingly muddled task, and it simply does not contribute much clarity to the dis-

---

Christ's lordship is necessary for saving faith but says that "in true faith there is an element of submission" (p. 17), and Harrison affirms that "Christ is Lord by virtue of resurrection whether anyone acknowledges it personally or not" (p. 16). The article would have focused the discussion more precisely if it had asked, "Is repentance from sin a necessary part of saving faith?" (Harrison: no; Stott: yes), and "Will good works and continuing to believe necessarily follow from saving faith?" (Harrison: no; Stott: yes).

[7] Charles Bing says, "Though both the Lordship Salvation position and the Free Grace position agree that Christ's Lordship is essential for salvation, there is disagreement over how an unsaved person must respond to Christ's Lordship in order to be saved. . . . Jesus is Lord of all regardless of one's submission to Him." *Lordship Salvation*, 178–79.

[8] John MacArthur says, "I am certain that while some understand more than others, no one who is saved fully understands all the implications of Jesus' lordship at the moment of conversion." But he adds, in distinction from the Free Grace position, "I am, however, equally certain that no one can be saved who is either unwilling to obey Christ or consciously, callously rebellious against His Lordship." *The Gospel According to Jesus: What Is Authentic Faith?*, anniversary ed. (Grand Rapids, MI: Zondervan, 2008), 15.

cussion. Therefore I do not plan to discuss the question of the lordship of Christ in the rest of this book. I do not think that is the best way to focus the issue.

In addition, when Free Grace proponents refer to the position that disagrees with them as the "Lordship Salvation" position, they wrongly suggest that it is an unusual or minority view that seeks to add the idea of lordship to the ordinary idea of salvation. But, in fact, what the Free Grace movement calls the "Lordship Salvation" view has just been the ordinary, mainstream, evangelical Protestant view since the Reformation. It is not a novel or minority view at all, for it has been held by all the main branches of Protestantism (see chapter 1).

My own conclusion is that there are important differences concerning two other matters:

1) whether repentance from sin (in the sense of remorse for sin and an internal resolve to forsake it) is necessary for saving faith, and

2) whether good works and continuing to believe necessarily follow from saving faith.

The two positions clearly and explicitly disagree on the answers to those questions. And it is on those two questions that the debate should be focused. In my judgment, any further discussion that refers to this as the "Lordship Salvation controversy" will just muddy the waters. In the material that follows, I will simply refer to the two positions as the "Free Grace" position and the "historic Protestant" position (or, at times, the "non–Free Grace" position).

At this point someone might ask why I refer to the position I am opposing as the "Free Grace" position. After all, don't all Protestants believe in free grace? My response is that, yes, all orthodox Protestants believe in free grace, but it is always courteous to refer to a position that you disagree with by a descriptive term that the other side would choose for itself, and the term "Free Grace" (capitalized) is commonly used by the two major organizations that promote this view, both the Free Grace Alliance[9] and the Grace Evangelical Society.[10]

By the same token, I hope that no reviewer of this book will refer to my position as the "Lordship Salvation" position, for I explicitly disavow that label as misleading and confusing (see above). Throughout this book, I regularly refer to my own position as the "historic Protestant" position (or sometimes as the "non–Free Grace" position), and I attempt to demonstrate in chapter 1 that I am arguing for the viewpoint held historically by the most influential leaders and statements of faith in the various branches of historic Protestantism, including representative Lutheran, Reformed, Anglican, Baptist, Methodist, and Pentecostal groups.[11]

However, my concerns with the Free Grace movement are not limited to theological differences on those two points above. I am convinced that the theological position held by the Free

[9] See their website: http://www.freegracealliance.com.

[10] See their website: http://www.faithalone.org. It is common in Christian circles to refer to groups by names they would take for themselves, such as "Baptists" (even though nearly all churches believe in baptism), or "Congregationalists" (even though all churches have congregations).

[11] Although my book *Systematic Theology* makes clear that I personally hold doctrines that would place me in the Reformed and Baptist theological traditions (with sympathy for some teachings of the charismatic movement), the position I am arguing for here is more "historic Protestant" than uniquely representative of any of those three traditions.

Grace movement is also inconsistent with *historic* Protestant convictions and has harmful consequences in the church today as well. Therefore, I have organized my concerns into five chapters, and in those chapters these two differences over repentance and good works will surface again and again. The first chapter deals with the history of Protestantism, and the remaining four deal with my concerns about the practical consequences of Free Grace teaching.

1

Not the "Faith Alone" of the Reformation

The Free Grace movement does not teach the Reformation doctrine of "justification by faith alone."

When people first hear Free Grace advocates say that they promote "justification by faith alone," it sounds attractive, because even Christians with little knowledge of theology remember that Protestants all hold to justification by faith alone. What is not clear at first is that the Free Grace movement teaches a novel and distorted view of justification by faith alone, a view that was never taught by the great leaders of the Protestant Reformation. In fact, at its very core the Free Grace movement is based on a misunderstanding of the way the word *alone* functions in the historic Protestant affirmations of justification by faith alone.

The historic Protestant position has often been summarized in a brief sentence:

> We are justified by faith *alone*, but the faith that justifies is *never alone*.

The second half of the sentence, "the faith that justifies is never alone," means that other things always accompany saving faith. In particular, saving faith is always followed by changes in a person's conduct of life. In other words, saving faith is never alone in a person, for *some good works will always accompany saving faith in a person's life* and will be seen after a person comes to faith.

Therefore the Reformers always took "faith alone" to mean that faith is the only thing that God responds to. But historic Protestant teaching from the Reformation onward has *never* taken "faith alone" to mean "faith that *occurs by itself* in a person, unaccompanied by other human activities" (the Free Grace view).

A. Protestant leaders throughout history have consistently disagreed with the Free Grace position.

When we examine the writings of the great Reformation teachers and confessions of faith, we find a consensus of teaching that we are justified by faith alone, but the faith that justifies is never alone in the life of a believer, because genuine saving faith will always be accompanied by good works that come after justification. Here are several examples:

1. John Calvin (1509–1564). (Calvin was the first and most influential theologian in the Reformed tradition.)

> Christ justifies no one whom he does not at the same time sanctify. . . . Thus it is clear how true it is that *we are justified not without works yet not through works*.[1]

---

[1] John Calvin, *Institutes of the Christian Religion*, 2 vols., trans. Ford Lewis Battles (Philadelphia: Westminster, 1960), 3.16.1; also found in the Henry Beveridge translation: John

In another place Calvin writes:

> I wish the reader to understand that as often as we mention faith alone in this question, we are not thinking of a dead faith, which worketh not by love, but holding faith to be the only cause of justification. (Galatians 5:6; Romans 3:22.) *It is therefore faith alone which justifies, and yet the faith which justifies is not alone*: just as it is the heat alone of the sun which warms the earth, and yet in the sun it is not alone, because it is constantly conjoined with light. Wherefore we do not separate the whole grace of regeneration from faith, but claim the power and faculty of justifying entirely for faith, as we ought.[2]

2. Formula of Concord (1576). (This is the great summary of Lutheran doctrine that expressed a consensus among differing Lutheran groups.)

> III. We believe, also, teach, and confess that *Faith alone is the means and instrument whereby we lay hold on Christ the Saviour*, and so in Christ lay hold on that righteousness which is able to stand before the judgment of God; for that faith, for Christ's sake, is imputed to us for righteousness (Rom. 5:5).

> VIII. We believe, teach, and confess that, although antecedent contrition and subsequent new obedience do not appertain to the article of justification before God, yet we are not to imagine any such justifying faith as can exist and

---

Calvin, *Institutes of the Christian Religion*, trans. Henry Beveridge (Peabody, MA: Hendrickson, 2008), 523; emphasis added.

[2] John Calvin, *Tracts and Letters: Acts of the Council of Trent, Antidote to the Canons of the Council of Trent*, Canon 11, accessed February 15, 2014, http://www.godrules.net /library/calvin/142calvin_c4.htm; emphasis added.

abide with a purpose of evil, to wit: of sinning and acting contrary to conscience. But after that man is justified by faith, then that true and living faith works by love, and good works always follow justifying faith, and are most certainly found together with it, provided only it be a true and living faith. For *true faith is never alone*, but hath always charity and hope in its train.[3]

3. Thirty-Nine Articles of the Church of England (1571). (This is the doctrinal standard of Anglican or Episcopalian churches.)

XII. Of Good Works: Albeit that Good Works, which are the fruits of Faith, and follow after Justification, cannot put away our sins, and endure the severity of God's judgment; yet are they pleasing and acceptable to God in Christ, and do spring out necessarily of a true and lively faith; insomuch that by them a lively Faith may be as evidently known as a tree discerned by the fruit.[4]

4. Westminster Confession of Faith (1646). (This is the doctrinal standard used by most Presbyterian and Reformed churches.)

11.2: Faith, thus receiving and resting on Christ and his righteousness, is the *alone* instrument of justification: yet is it *not alone* in the person justified, but is ever accompanied with all other saving graces, and is no dead faith, but worketh by love.[5]

---

[3] *The Creeds of Christendom*, ed. Philip Schaff, 3 vols. (1931; repr. Grand Rapids, MI: Baker, 1983), 3:116, 118; emphasis added.
[4] Ibid., 3:494; emphasis added.
[5] Ibid., 3:626; emphasis added.

5. New Hampshire Baptist Confession (1833).
(This statement has been widely used by various
Baptist groups in the United States.)

> VII. Regeneration . . . is effected . . . by the power of the
> Holy Spirit . . . its proper evidence appears in the holy fruits
> of repentance, and faith, and newness of life.

> VIII. We believe that Repentance and Faith are sacred du-
> ties, and also inseparable graces, wrought in our souls by
> the regenerating Spirit of God; whereby being deeply con-
> vinced of our guilt, danger, and helplessness, and of the
> way of salvation by Christ, we turn to God with unfeigned
> contrition, confession, and supplication for mercy; at the
> same time heartily receiving the Lord Jesus Christ as our
> Prophet, Priest, and King, and relying on him alone as the
> only and all sufficient Saviour.[6]

6. John Wesley (1703–1791). (Wesley was the founder of
Methodism.)

> We are, doubtless, justified by faith. This is the corner-stone
> of the whole Christian building. We are justified without the
> works of the law, as any previous condition of justification;
> but they are an immediate fruit of that faith whereby we
> are justified. So that if good works do not follow our faith,
> even all inward and outward holiness, it is plain our faith
> is nothing worth; we are yet in our sins.[7]

---

[6] Ibid., 3:744–45.
[7] John Wesley, "The Law Established Through Faith," in *The Sermons of John Wesley*, accessed November 16, 2014, http://wesley.nnu.edu/john-wesley/the-sermons-of-john-wesley
-1872-edition/sermon-35-the-law-established-through-faith-discourse-one/.

7. Assemblies of God Statement of Fundamental Truths (1916). (This is one of the oldest and largest Pentecostal denominations.)

> Salvation is received through repentance toward God and faith toward the Lord Jesus Christ. By the washing of regeneration and renewing of the Holy Spirit, being justified by grace through faith, man becomes an heir of God according to the hope of eternal life (Luke 24:47; John 3:3; Romans 10:13-15; Ephesians 2:8; Titus 2:11; 3:5-7). . . . The inward evidence of salvation is the direct witness of the Spirit (Romans 8:16). The outward evidence to all men is a life of righteousness and true holiness (Ephesians 4:24; Titus 2:12).[8]

B. Therefore, the Free Grace movement today is not upholding the Reformation doctrine of *sola fide*, or "justification by faith alone."

When we read this consistent testimony from all of the major traditions that flowed out of the Reformation—Lutheran, Reformed and Presbyterian, Anglican, Baptist, Methodist, and Pentecostal—we begin to wonder where Free Grace advocates ever found their unusual view of justification by faith alone. It simply does not represent the view of any of the mainstream evangelical Protestant groups that followed the Reformation. None of them ever taught that "justification by faith alone" means "faith that is not accompanied by repentance or by good works." In the historic Protestant theological tradition, "faith alone" has never meant "faith not accompanied by other human

---

[8] "Assemblies of God Statement of Fundamental Truths," sec. 5, accessed June 23, 2015, http://agchurches.org/Sitefiles/Default/RSS/AG.org%20TOP/Beliefs/SFT_2011.pdf.

actions." Rather, "faith alone" has always meant that "faith is the only thing that God responds to with the act of justification."

This insistence that genuine faith *must be accompanied by good works* becomes all the more striking when we recognize that the leaders of the Reformation were deeply concerned to separate faith from works done to merit salvation. They insisted that faith did not need to be accompanied by such works, in distinction from their Catholic opponents who taught that justification required faith plus participation in the sacraments—we are saved by *faith plus* being baptized, attending the Roman Catholic mass, doing penance, and so forth[9]—all of which, in the eyes of the Protestant leaders, were *works* to earn merit with God.

The leaders of the Reformation were not trying to separate faith from genuine repentance from sin. Nor were they saying that genuine faith could occur without a change in someone's life—they repeatedly said it could not!

Were the Reformers guilty then of adding works to faith as the basis of justification? Absolutely not! They were in the midst of a life-and-death struggle for the very survival of the true gospel and the very life of the church. At the heart of their struggle was *sola fide*, "faith alone." They were willing to die rather than add works to faith as the means of justification. Yet they repeatedly and unanimously insisted that justification

---

[9] The seven Roman Catholic sacraments are (1) baptism, (2) confirmation, (3) eucharist (what Protestants call the "Lord's Supper"), (4) penance, (5) anointing of the sick, (6) holy orders (that is, ordination to be a priest or a nun), and (7) matrimony. See *Catechism of the Catholic Church*, 2nd ed. (New York: Doubleday, 1997), para. 1,113. The *Catechism* goes on to say, "The Church affirms that for believers the sacraments of the New Covenant are necessary for salvation" (para. 1,129); and, "Justification is not only the remission of sins, but also the sanctification and renewal of the interior man" (para. 1,989).

is by faith alone, but the faith that justifies is never alone—it is always accompanied by good works.

I think the initial attractiveness of the Free Grace movement is that at first it *sounds* to people like it is promoting a Reformation doctrine. In reality, it is promoting a doctrine that the leaders of the Reformation had nothing to do with. It is promoting a novel view in the history of Protestantism.[10]

Therefore, what is its proof? The proof comes not from the history of the Reformation or Protestantism, in which the key teaching was justification by faith alone. The Free Grace view must find its support only from the claim that the New Testament teaches this view. But where is it in the New Testament? Where does the New Testament ever say that saving faith can occur by itself in a person who is saved, without repentance from sin and without good works following? I think nowhere.

On the other hand, there is much New Testament teaching that many changes will necessarily come once one believes in Christ: "Therefore, if anyone is in Christ, *he is a new creation.* The old has passed away; behold, the new has come" (2 Cor. 5:17). And Paul does not say, "You were justified but nothing else happened when you believed." Rather, after naming a long list of sins, Paul declares that their lives have decisively changed:

---

[10] However, the Free Grace view of saving faith is similar to that of the eighteenth-century Sandemanians, named after their leader Robert Sandeman (1718–1771), a Scottish pastor, who held that "bare assent to the work of Christ is alone necessary." R. E. D. Clark, "Sandemanians," *New International Dictionary of the Christian Church*, ed. J. D. Douglas (Grand Rapids, MI: Zondervan, 1974), 877. Sandemanian churches were established in both the UK and the US, but Sandeman's successors "never had more than a small following." "Glasites (also Sandemanians)" in *Oxford Dictionary of the Christian Church*, ed. F. L. Cross (Oxford, UK: Oxford University Press, 1974), 571.

> And such were some of you. But you were washed, you were
> sanctified, you were justified in the name of the Lord Jesus
> Christ and by the Spirit of our God. (1 Cor. 6:11)

Many other passages teach that regeneration, which always
occurs in close connection with saving faith, brings numerous
significant changes in a person's life.[11]

C. There is no logical difficulty in claiming this.

Free Grace supporters sometimes claim that it is a contradiction
to claim that we are justified by faith alone, but the faith that
justifies is never alone. For example, in a book promoted by the
Free Grace Alliance, author Fred Lybrand examines this claim in
the form, "It is therefore faith alone which justifies, and yet the
faith which justifies is not alone." Lybrand says that this claim
is "internally incongruent" and that it "leads to the notion that
faith alone = faith not alone."[12] Lybrand adds that the illogical
character of this claim can be stated in other ways, such as:

> Faith apart from works = Faith with (not apart from) works.

Or:

> Faith without works = Faith never without works.[13]

But Lybrand repeatedly fails to give adequate consideration to
the two different verbs in the two halves of the sentence,

---

[11] See Wayne Grudem, *Systematic Theology* (Grand Rapids, MI: Zondervan, 1994), 704–6.
[12] Fred R. Lybrand, *Back to Faith: Reclaiming Gospel Clarity in an Age of Incongruence* (Maitland, FL: Xulon Press, 2009), 1–19.
[13] Ibid., 21. Fred Chay and John Correia say, "If we are to articulate that we are saved by faith alone and then stipulate by definition that the faith that saves is never alone, it seems difficult to then pronounce that we are saved by faith alone, since by definition faith is never alone." They imply that this violates "the law of non-contradiction." Fred Chay and John Correia, *The Faith That Saves* (Dallas: Grace Line, 2008), 150.

> We are *justified* by faith alone,
> but the faith that justifies *is* never alone.

The two different verbs make clear that "faith alone" in the first half of the expression is functioning in a different way from "faith alone" in the second half. In the first half "faith alone" modifies "justified," and in the second half it modifies "is." When Lybrand and others in the Free Grace movement remove both verbs, then of course they can produce what looks like a contradiction: "faith alone and not faith alone." But when they remove the verbs in this way, they distort the meaning of this doctrinal summary, and they repeatedly fail to understand the sentence in the way it is intended.

A contradiction would be seen if we put the same verb in both halves of the sentence:

> We *are justified* by faith alone, and we *are not justified* by faith alone.

But no significant Protestant leader since the Reformation has ever said that. And no statement of faith since the Reformation has ever said that. Another contradiction would be:

> The faith that justifies *is* by itself, and the faith that justifies *is not* by itself.

But none of the Protestant Reformers ever said that. Nor did they ever mean that. They said exactly what they meant: We are justified by faith alone, and the faith that justifies is not alone.

By ignoring the crucial difference in verbs in the two halves of the sentence, Lybrand even claims—in a book promoted by the Free Grace Alliance—that he has found the same "logical flaw" in John Calvin, Martin Luther, the Westminster Confession of Faith, John Owen, John Wesley, George Whitefield, Jonathan Edwards, Charles Spurgeon, Charles Hodge, J. Gresham Machen, Louis Berkhof, J. I. Packer, John Piper, R. C. Sproul, Billy Graham, and others—indeed, almost the whole history of Protestantism![14]

He is surprised that he has found so little literature "specifically challenging this cliché."[15] His explanation for this lack of critical analysis is that this common summary was just accepted as "an idiom, a cliché, or a proverb" that was simply taken as an "unquestioned assumption."[16]

But for Lybrand to claim a logical difficulty here is to claim that hundreds of the greatest minds in the history of the church since the Reformation and tens of thousands of the brightest pastors have failed to notice a *simple* logical fallacy at the heart of their faith. Not to put it too strongly, this is unlikely. It is more likely that the critic has not understood the sentence in the sense in which it is intended.

A simple example is helpful in illustrating how the Reformation teaching is not a contradiction.

This illustration of my key ring from Phoenix Seminary shows the

---

[14] Lybrand, *Back to Faith*, 5–9.
[15] *Cliché* is the term Lybrand repeatedly uses to refer to the doctrinal summary "We are justified by faith alone, but the faith that justifies is never alone."
[16] Lybrand, *Back to Faith*, 7–8.

two different senses in which "alone" can be used. Now it is perfectly true to say that my office door is *opened by the blue key alone* (it is the only key that works to open that door). But the blue key is *never by itself*, because I always keep it on the key ring with the yellow key (which opens the faculty office corridor), the plain key (which opens the classroom doors), and the small key (which opens the computer door at the podium where I teach). Therefore my office door is opened by the blue key alone (it is the only key that works), but the blue key that opens my office door is never alone (it is never found by itself but is always accompanied by other keys).

This simple statement about my keys is parallel to the historic Reformation teaching that we are justified by faith alone (faith is the only response that God requires from us), but the faith that justifies is never alone (because it never occurs by itself, but is always accompanied by—or includes—repentance from sin and is always followed by other actions such as doing good works and continuing to believe).

D. Why is the proper meaning of "justification by faith alone" so important?

I have spent several pages on this first point, explaining what it means that we are "justified by faith alone," because I think a misunderstanding of this issue has led Free Grace supporters to all the other mistakes I raise concerns about in the following pages.

Why do Free Grace advocates claim that we should not tell unbelievers that they need to repent of their sins when they come to trust in Christ? Because they think this is adding another element (repentance) to "faith alone." (See the discussion in chapter 2.)

Why do Free Grace advocates claim that we should not say that good works are a necessary result of saving faith? Because they think that this is adding another element (good works) to "faith alone." And why do they claim that we should not say that a true believer will continue to believe until the end of his or her life? Because they think this also adds another element (continuing in faith) to "faith alone." (See discussion in chapter 3.)

Why do some Free Grace advocates teach that saving faith is only intellectual agreement with some facts about Jesus and does not also include heartfelt trust in Jesus *as a person*? And why do other Free Grace advocates speak of trust in Jesus as a person but do not emphasize it? Because they think this would be adding another element (personal encounter with Christ) to "faith alone." (See discussion in chapter 4.)

Why do Free Grace advocates adopt highly unusual and unprecedented interpretations of numerous New Testament texts that speak, on the surface, of the need for repentance or the necessary evidence of good works and continuing in faith? Because they need to explain away those verses that seem to them to be adding other elements to "faith alone." (See discussion in chapter 5.)

But if Free Grace advocates are wrong in their understanding of justification by faith alone—that is, if their view is not the view that was taught by leaders of the Reformation (as I have argued above), and if it is not the view of saving faith taught by the New Testament (as I will argue in subsequent chapters)—then the entire Free Grace movement is based on a mistake, and it should be abandoned.

2

No Call to Repent of Sins

Free Grace theology weakens the gospel message by avoiding any call to unbelievers to repent of their sins.

A. Repentance from sin in the New Testament

1. Repentance from sin in many key summaries of the gospel

A call to repentance is found in several gospel summaries in the New Testament. For example, when the author of Hebrews wants to mention foundational Christian doctrines, he includes repentance and faith:

> Therefore let us leave the elementary doctrine of Christ and go on to maturity, not laying again a foundation of *repentance* from [Gk. *apo*] dead works and of *faith* toward God. (Heb. 6:1)

In this verse, the "from" (Greek *apo*) is important: it shows that repentance here is not merely a "change of mind" about one's accountability before God (a common Free Grace explanation[1]) but includes a conscious turning *away from* dead works. This implies a decision to turn away from one's former pattern of life and begin to walk in a path of obedience to Christ.[2]

Therefore this verse is one of many examples of repentance in the sense that I have defined it elsewhere:

> Repentance is a heartfelt sorrow for sin, a renouncing of it, and a sincere commitment to forsake it and walk in obedience to Christ.[3]

This is not adding works to faith. Rather, repentance and faith are mentioned together in Hebrews 6:1 because repentance *from* sin is a component of truly turning *to* Christ in faith for salvation from that very sin. Such a commitment of the heart to turn from sin is no more "salvation by works" than is a commitment of the heart to trust in Christ. Both are decisions of the heart. Neither one is a *work* in the sense of an act one does to merit favor with God.

Several other verses also mention repentance as an important part of evangelistic proclamations of the gospel of Christ:

> . . . and that *repentance and forgiveness of sins* should be proclaimed in his name to all nations, beginning from Jerusalem. (Luke 24:47)

---

[1] I discuss different Free Grace explanations of repentance below, pp. 55–70.

[2] The same idea of turning from sin and turning toward God is found in Paul's description of what happened when the Thessalonians came to saving faith: "You turned *to God from idols* to serve the living and true God" (1 Thess. 1:9) (though the word *repentance* is not used here).

[3] Wayne Grudem, *Systematic Theology* (Grand Rapids, MI: Zondervan, 1994), 713.

This is Jesus's summary, after his resurrection, of the gospel message that his disciples would proclaim throughout the world, and "repentance and forgiveness of sins" are explicitly mentioned as the content of the preaching. Notice here that faith is not even mentioned explicitly. Just as genuine saving faith assumes that a person has repented from sin, so genuine repentance assumes that someone is turning to Christ in faith. Repentance from sin and faith in Christ are two sides of the same coin, two aspects of the same decision of the heart.

Several summaries of gospel preaching in the book of Acts include the need for repentance as part of the gospel that was preached:

> And Peter said to them, "*Repent* and be baptized every one of you in the name of Jesus Christ for the forgiveness of your sins, and you will receive the gift of the Holy Spirit. (Acts 2:38)

(Faith is not even named in this verse but is assumed to be implied when genuine repentance is present.)

> *Repent* therefore, and turn back, that your sins may be blotted out. (Acts 3:19)

> God exalted him at his right hand as Leader and Savior, to give *repentance* to Israel and forgiveness of sins. (Acts 5:31)

> When they heard these things they fell silent. And they glorified God, saying, "Then to the Gentiles also God has granted *repentance* that leads to life." (Acts 11:18)

In Acts 11:18 the Jerusalem Christians rejoice because the gospel has begun to come with power even to Gentiles. And they summarize this not by saying that God has granted to the Gentiles to "believe in Christ" (which would also be true theologically), but that God has granted the Gentiles "repentance that leads to life."

Paul's evangelistic preaching regularly includes a call to repentance, as is evident in his speech to the philosophers on the Areopagus in Athens:

> The times of ignorance God overlooked, but now he commands all people everywhere *to repent*, because he has fixed a day on which he will judge the world in righteousness by a man whom he has appointed; and of this he has given assurance to all by raising him from the dead. (Acts 17:30–31)

Paul is speaking here about repentance from one's sins, not merely a change of opinion or change of mind, because the second half of the sentence warns of a final judgment "in righteousness." Repentance from sins is the way one escapes from a judgment based on moral right and wrong, a judgment "in righteousness."

When summarizing his gospel message to the city of Ephesus, Paul said it this way:

> . . . testifying both to Jews and to Greeks of *repentance toward God* and of faith in our Lord Jesus Christ. (Acts 20:21)

Both repentance and faith are mentioned in this passage. This particular Greek construction ties repentance and faith closely together, for only one definite article governs both nouns.[4] This suggests that we should regard repentance and faith as two closely connected parts of one overall action, parts that cannot be separated.

In addition, this verse mentions repentance "toward God" (Greek *eis theon*). This means it must be a repentance that involves personally turning *toward* him and coming into his presence. Yet to come into the presence of the living, omnipotent, infinitely holy Creator of the universe would be impossible without a decision to turn from one's sins and plead for forgiveness.

For example, when Isaiah "saw the Lord sitting upon a throne, high and lifted up," he cried out, "Woe is me! For I am lost; for I am a man of unclean lips, and I dwell in the midst of a people of unclean lips; for my eyes have seen the King, the LORD of hosts!" (Isa. 6:15). And when Peter saw Christ's majesty demonstrated with a miraculously large catch of fish, "he fell down at Jesus' knees, saying, 'Depart from me, for I am a sinful man, O Lord'" (Luke 5:8). "Repentance toward God" necessarily involves repentance from one's sin.

This is why these summaries of gospel preaching in the New Testament include a component of repentance from one's sins. The gospel call, according to the New Testament, is ever and always a call to turn away from your sin as you turn toward

---

[4] The Greek text is: διαμαρτυρόμενος Ἰουδαίοις τε καὶ ῞Ελλησιν τὴν εἰς θεὸν μετάνοιαν καὶ πίστιν εἰς τὸν κύριον ἡμῶν Ἰησοῦν Χριστόν (Acts 20:21), which may be translated in a woodenly literal way as "testifying to both Jews and Greeks of the toward-God repentance and faith in our Lord Jesus." This is an example of Sharp's Rule, indicating some kind of unity between the two nouns; see discussion in Daniel Wallace, *Greek Grammar beyond the Basics* (Grand Rapids, MI: Zondervan, 1996), 289; see also his larger discussion of this construction, 270–90.

the Lord to seek forgiveness from him. Here is the beautiful wording of Isaiah's invitation:

> Seek the LORD while he may be found;
>> call upon him while he is near;
> let the wicked forsake his way,
>> and the unrighteous man his thoughts;
> let him return to the LORD, that he may have compassion
>> on him,
>> and to our God, for he will abundantly pardon.
>> (Isa. 55:6–7)

Paul had another opportunity to summarize his gospel message to both Jews and Greeks when standing before King Agrippa:

> Therefore, O King Agrippa, I was not disobedient to the heavenly vision, but declared first to those in Damascus, then in Jerusalem and throughout all the region of Judea, and also to the Gentiles, that they should *repent* and *turn to God*, performing deeds in keeping with their repentance. (Acts 26:19–20)

This summary of Paul's gospel presentation includes both repentance and turning to God, but again, faith is not even named explicitly. Paul's mention of "performing deeds in keeping with their repentance" indicates that a changed pattern of life is expected to follow, and that implies that once again repentance *from one's sins*, not merely a change of mind about certain theological matters, is in view.

> The Lord is not slow to fulfill his promise as some count slowness, but is patient toward you, not wishing that

any should perish, but that all should reach *repentance.*
(2 Pet. 3:9)[5]

For unbelievers to be saved, Peter says that it is necessary that
they should "reach repentance."

2. Repentance from sin in narrative examples
of Jesus dealing with individuals

The need for repentance from one's sins is clearly affirmed
by some of Jesus's encounters with unbelievers. For example,
when he met the rich young ruler, he asked him to give up the
primary idol that was keeping his heart from following Christ:
"Sell all that you have and distribute to the poor, and you will
have treasure in heaven; and come, follow me" (Luke 18:22).

But when Jesus talked to the Samaritan woman at the well,
he challenged her regarding cohabiting with a man to whom
she was not married:

> Jesus said to her, "Go, call your husband, and come here."
> The woman answered him, "I have no husband." Jesus
> said to her, "You are right in saying, 'I have no husband';
> for you have had five husbands, and the one you now have
> is not your husband. What you have said is true." (John
> 4:16–18)

In a third case, the tax collector Zacchaeus, who had been
stealing money from people, showed signs of genuine repentance from previous sins and therefore true conversion:

---

[5] When Peter says that God "is patient toward you," the sense of "you" is broad and
includes unbelievers among Peter's hearers, such as the "false teachers among you," and
their followers, in 2:1–3, and the "scoffers" in 3:3. It also includes those whom Peter tells
to "confirm your calling and election" in 1:10.

And Zacchaeus stood and said to the Lord, "Behold, Lord, the half of my goods I give to the poor. And if I have defrauded anyone of anything, I restore it fourfold." And Jesus said to him, "Today salvation has come to this house." (Luke 19:8–9)[6]

3. Repentance from sin in Protestant confessions of faith

Because of the frequent inclusions of repentance as an essential part of the New Testament gospel message, it is not surprising that some Protestant groups have included the need for repentance in their statements of faith. The Westminster Confession of Faith (1643–1646) says that in repentance a sinner "so grieves for, and hates his sins, as to turn from them all unto God, purposing and endeavoring to walk with him in all the ways of his commandments," and, further, that repentance "is of such necessity to all sinners, that none may expect pardon without it" (15.2–3). The Baptist Faith and Message (Southern Baptist Convention, 1925; revised 1963, 2000) says,

Repentance and faith are inseparable experiences of grace. Repentance is a genuine turning from sin toward God. Faith is the acceptance of Jesus Christ and commitment of the entire personality to Him as Lord and Saviour. Justification is God's gracious and full acquittal upon principles of His righteousness of all sinners who repent and believe in Christ. (4.A)

---

[6] The need for repentance is made clear in several other examples of Jesus's encounters with individual people. John MacArthur Jr. analyzes many of these passages in his helpful book *The Gospel According to Jesus: What Is Authentic Faith?*, anniversary ed. (Grand Rapids, MI: Zondervan, 2008).

4. Why is repentance not mentioned in John's Gospel?

In spite of all these verses showing that repentance was a key part of early gospel presentations, Free Grace supporters emphasize that John's Gospel is the most evangelistic Gospel in the New Testament, and there is no mention of repentance; only the need to believe in Jesus. Zane Hodges writes,

> The fourth gospel says nothing at all about repentance, much less does it connect repentance in any way with eternal life. This fact is the death knell for lordship theology. Only a resolute blindness can resist the obvious conclusion: *John did not regard repentance as a condition for eternal life.* If he had, he would have said so. After all, that's what his book is all about: obtaining eternal life (John 20:30–31).[7]

In reply, several points can be made.

1) Hodges makes a very basic and serious mistake when he attempts to base a doctrine on only one book of Scripture. The early church rightly condemned the teachings of Marcion (c. AD 85–160), whose canon of Scripture included only eleven books (no Old Testament, and in the New Testament only a shortened Gospel of Luke and ten of Paul's thirteen epistles).[8] But here Hodges is basing his doctrine of saving faith on only one book in the Bible, the Gospel of John, and implying that people are wrong to refer to the teachings of any other book of the Bible in defining saving faith.

That is simply incorrect theological reasoning. If other verses

---

[7] Zane Hodges, *Absolutely Free! A Biblical Reply to Lordship Salvation* (Grand Rapids, MI: Zondervan, 1989), 148; emphasis original.

[8] See Gregg Allison, *Historical Theology* (Grand Rapids, MI: Zondervan, 2011), 41–42.

in other books of the Bible give us further teaching about the nature of saving faith, then we should use those verses as well to help us understand faith. These other verses are also part of "all Scripture," which is given to us by God to be "profitable for teaching, for reproof, for correction, and for training in righteousness" (2 Tim. 3:16).

2) The need for repentance on the part of those who trust in Jesus is repeatedly made clear in Matthew, Mark, and Luke. Should the teachings and actions of Jesus in these Gospels play no role in our understanding of what the gospel message should include? Consider these passages:

> Jesus came into Galilee, proclaiming the gospel of God, and saying, "The time is fulfilled, and the kingdom of God is at hand; repent and believe in the gospel." (Mark 1:14–15)

> I have not come to call the righteous but sinners to repentance. (Luke 5:32)

> No, I tell you; but unless you repent, you will all likewise perish. (Luke 13:3)

> Just so, I tell you, there will be more joy in heaven over one sinner who repents than over ninety-nine righteous persons who need no repentance. (Luke 15:7)

In addition, at the very end of Luke, there is Jesus's great summary of what gospel the disciples would preach when he sent them out:

> Thus it is written, that the Christ should suffer and on the third day rise from the dead, and that repentance and

forgiveness of sins should be proclaimed in his name to all nations, beginning from Jerusalem. (Luke 24:46–47)

3) It is likely that John's Gospel assumes the background of the teaching in Matthew, Mark, and Luke, and these three Gospels contain much teaching about repentance (see above, for only a few of many verses). John's Gospel seems to have been written fairly late in the first century AD, and if we accept traditional authorship of Matthew, Mark, and Luke, then John was written after these Gospels were already circulating. This means that John never intended his Gospel to stand alone, apart from Matthew, Mark, and Luke.

Arguments about the relationship between John and the Synoptic Gospels are detailed and complex, but Donald Guthrie says that the theory that "has most to be said for it and is most generally accepted" is that John is "supplementary to . . . the [Synoptic Gospels]." He adds that "John often avoids unnecessary duplication, so that it would seem he assumes his readers will be acquainted with the Synoptic records. . . . It is reasonable to suppose that it was composed with the others in mind. . . . This view is tenable even if it be maintained that John did not use the Synoptic Gospels as a source."[9] This would explain why John omits so many significant events in Jesus's life.[10] And this

---

[9] Donald Guthrie, *New Testament Introduction* (Downers Grove, IL: InterVarsity Press, 1970), 298. He has an extensive discussion of the relationship between John and the Synoptic Gospels on 287–300.

  Even if someone believes that John was not assuming his readers had access to the written Synoptic Gospels, John would surely have assumed that his readers were familiar with the oral traditions of Jesus's teachings, which were widely circulated.

[10] Guthrie notes that "John does not record the virgin birth, the baptism, temptation or transfiguration of Jesus, the cure of any demoniacs or lepers, the parables, the institution of the Lord's supper, the agony in the garden, the cry of dereliction, or the ascension." Guthrie, *New Testament Introduction*, 288.

is another argument for giving strong consideration not just to John but also to Matthew, Mark, and Luke when we seek to know whether repentance is a necessary part of saving faith.

4) The book of Acts contains many summaries of how the early church preached the gospel. Should we not learn from the apostles themselves what *the content of the gospel* should include? But the book of Acts contains many calls to repentance in its summaries of the basic evangelistic message preached by the apostles and the rest of the early church (see pp. 43–46 above, for discussion of Acts 2:38; 3:19; 5:31; 11:18; 17:30–31; 20:21; 26:19–20).

5) Turning back to John's Gospel itself, we find several indications that he assumed repentance would be an essential part of what it means to believe in Jesus.

a) Jesus taught that the role of the Holy Spirit would be to "convict the world concerning sin and righteousness and judgment" (John 16:8), yet a conviction of *sin* is for the purpose of leading people to repent of their sin.

b) In the story of the woman at the well and Samaria, when Jesus tells the woman, "Go, call your husband, and come here" (John 4:16), the narrative shows that he is calling her to repentance for her sexual immorality.

c) John explains belief in Jesus with many images which imply a close personal encounter with him who is the living Lord and God of the universe, such as "coming to Christ" (John 6:35, 37, 44; 7:37), "receiving" Christ (John 1:11–12), "believing in (or into)" Christ (John 3:16, and many other passages), drinking the water that Christ gives (John 4:14), and even eating his flesh and drinking his blood (John 6:53–56). Such close, personal interaction is unthinkable for any sinner apart from deep, heartfelt repentance for one's sins.

d) Because the New Testament authors thought of repentance and faith as two different aspects of the same action, they could refer to that action in different ways: sometimes by speaking of both repentance and faith (Acts 20:21; Heb. 6:1), sometimes by speaking of repentance alone (Mark 6:12; Luke 13:3; 24:27; Acts 2:38; 3:19; 5:31; 11:18; 17:30; 26:19–20), and sometimes by speaking of faith or "believing" alone (Acts 4:4; Rom. 10:9–11; Gal. 2:16; and frequently in John's Gospel and elsewhere). This pattern of many New Testament verses shows that in contexts that speak of a person's initial conversion to Christ, when either repentance alone or faith alone is mentioned, the other one is implied even when it is not made explicit.

e) Many things that Jesus teaches in John's Gospel imply that those who believe in him have indeed repented of their sins, because they have turned from their previous pattern of life and they now "follow" Jesus as a sheep follows its shepherd (John 1:43; 10:4, 27). A believer is one who turns from his evil deeds and "comes to the light, so that it may be clearly seen that his works have been carried out in God" (John 3:21).

John MacArthur has compiled a longer list of characteristics of true believers according to John's Gospel:

> Although John never uses *repent* as a verb, the verbs he *does* employ are even stronger. He teaches that all true believers love the light (3:19), come to the light (3:20–21), obey the Son (3:36), practice the truth (3:21), worship in spirit and truth (4:23–24), honor God (5:22–24), do

good deeds (5:29), eat Jesus' flesh and drink His blood (6:48–66), love God (8:42, cf. 1 John 2:15), follow Jesus (10:26–28), and keep Jesus' commandments (14:15). . . . All of them presuppose repentance, commitment, and a desire to obey.

As those terms suggest, the apostle was careful to describe conversion as a complete turnabout. To John, becoming a believer meant resurrection from death to life, a coming out of darkness and into light, abandoning lies for the truth, exchanging hatred for love, and forsaking the world for God. What are those but images of radical conversion?[11]

6) Arguments that take the form of "this book of the Bible doesn't use this particular word" do not carry much weight. Several other important theological words are also missing from John, such as *pray, prayer, justification, atonement, sacrifice, ransom,* and *redeem.* In fact, except for John 20:23 (which is not a statement of the gospel) the terms *forgive* and *forgiveness* are not found in John. Should we then say that our evangelism should not include any of these ideas either? No, of course not.

To take another example, the word *love* does not occur in the book of Acts, which tells us about the life of the early church. Should we conclude from that that we should never discuss love when teaching how the church should act today? No, of course not. "This word is missing in this book" is just a misleading kind of argument and should be dismissed. We

---

[11] John MacArthur Jr., "Repentance in the Gospel of John," *Grace to You* website, accessed March 28, 2015, http://www.gty.org/resources/print/articles/A238.

should use every relevant passage in the whole Bible to define the nature of saving faith.

B. Two different Free Grace explanations for the "repentance" verses

Free Grace supporters provide two different explanations for the verses about repentance.

1) Some say *repentance* means "a change of mind" that is necessary for saving faith.

2) Others say *repentance* means "an inward resolve to turn from sin" that is an optional part of the Christian life.[12]

1. A necessary "change of mind"

The first Free Grace definition of *repentance*, one which seems to be more common, claims that *repentance* means just a "change of mind" (and not any internal resolve to turn from sin).

According to this Free Grace definition, when an unbeliever repents, he begins to think of himself as a sinner in need of salvation and begins to think of Christ as his Savior who has earned salvation for him by his death and resurrection. *Repentance* is thus a change of mind that is necessary for saving faith. But it need not imply any resolve to turn from one's sins. Charles Bing holds this view. He writes,

> The English word "repent" is used to translate the Greek word *metanoeō*. . . . The basic meaning of the Greek word

---

[12] Some Free Grace advocates may object that they do not think repentance is merely "optional" because they teach that it is desirable and important, though not required for salvation. But something that is not required is still optional.

metanoeō is "to change the mind." . . . Thus it is concluded that the word *metanoeō* denotes basically a change of mind.[13]

In order to evaluate Bing's "change of mind" definition, in the next two sections we need to examine evidence from Greek lexicons and from English translations of the Bible.

A. THE EVIDENCE FROM GREEK LEXICONS COMPARED TO CHARLES BING'S CITATIONS

Charles Bing says that "the basic meaning of the Greek word *metanoeō* is 'to change the mind,'" and as support he claims that "this is the uniform opinion of lexicographers and Lordship proponents alike."[14] But it does not appear that he has given his readers a fair or accurate report of the reference works that he quotes.

To demonstrate that lexicons (specialized Greek dictionaries) show the meaning "change of mind," Bing gives this footnote: "*BAGD*, s.v. '*metanoeō*,' 513."[15] This is a reference to the standard academic dictionary for New Testament Greek.[16] What Bing fails to tell his readers is that "change one's mind" is just the first possible meaning of *metanoeō*, and that the editors of the BAGD

---

[13] Charles Bing, *Lordship Salvation: A Biblical Evaluation and Response*, 2nd GraceLife ed. (Maitland, FL: Xulon Press, 2010), 67, 69. Bing notes that his book "was originally presented as a Ph.D. doctoral dissertation at Dallas Theological Seminary" (*iii*). In a later publication, Bing says that "it is also accurate to translate the word repentance as a *change of heart*." Charles Bing, *Grace, Salvation, and Discipleship: How to Understand Some Difficult Bible Passages* (The Woodlands, TX: Grace Theology Press, 2015), 51. However, he is still unwilling to include the essential element of an inward resolve to forsake sin in his explanation but says, "Obviously, and interchange should result in an outward change—that would be natural and expected, but it is not automatic" (52).

[14] Ibid., 67.

[15] Ibid., 67n28.

[16] The abbreviation BAGD refers to *A Greek-English Lexicon of the New Testament and Other Early Christian Literature*, ed. Walter Bauer, trans. William Arndt, F. Wilbur Gingrich, and Frederick W. Danker (Chicago: University of Chicago Press, 1979). The phrase Bing quotes is on p. 511, not 513.

lexicon do not put *any* New Testament passages in this first category. Rather, they put *every* New Testament passage under the second meaning, "feel remorse, repent, be converted (in religio-ethical sense)." They then go on to give many New Testament examples, and they include this statement: "Since in *metanoeō* the negative impulse of turning away is dominant, it is also used with *apo tinos* [from something]: repent and turn away from something (examples given include repenting from wickedness, from lawlessness, and, with the similar phrase *ek tinos*, repenting of murders, sorceries, sexual immorality, and thefts)."[17]

Therefore, while Bing leads his readers to believe that the standard Greek lexicon defines this term as "change one's mind," that is not the meaning this lexicon gives to it for any New Testament examples. And Bing does not mention that instead it gives a much stronger sense that includes feeling remorse, being converted, and turning away from sin, in a religious-ethical sense and in view of responsibility to God.

That is not the only difficulty with Bing's discussion of *metanoeō*, because he then goes on with a long quotation from the article on the words *metanoeō* ("repent") and *metanoia* ("repentance") in the multivolume reference work *Theological Dictionary of the New Testament* (*TDNT*),[18] volume 4, in the section written by Johannes Behm. Bing quotes a sentence from

---

[17] BAGD, 512. Because Charles Bing quoted the 1979 edition, abbreviated as BAGD, I have also quoted from that edition. The more recent edition from 2000, abbreviated BDAG, includes all the material on *metanoeō* that I have quoted from the 1979 edition and also adds, under the cognate noun *metanoia*, "repentance," this explanation: "in our literature with focus on the need of change in view of responsibility to deity" (640). "Our literature" in BDAG refers to the Greek literature that is the primary subject of this lexicon, namely, the New Testament and other early Christian literature.

[18] *Theological Dictionary of the New Testament*, 10 vols., ed. G. Kittel and G. Friedrich, trans. Geoffrey W. Bromiley (Grand Rapids, MI: Eerdmans, 1964–1976).

Behm that seems to give support to his proposed Free Grace meaning, "change of mind":

> For the Greeks *metanoeō* never suggests an alteration in the total moral attitude, a profound change in life's direction, a conversion which affects the whole conduct.[19]

Then Charles Bing says, "It is remarkable that Behm follows this analysis with the statement, 'One searches the Greek world in vain for the origin of the New Testament understanding of *metanoeō* and *metanoia*' (4:980)," and then Bing adds his own comment: "As if the New Testament writers were from *another world!*"[20]

What I find troubling here is that Bing fails to tell his readers, many of whom will fail to look up and read the long article in *TDNT*, that the *TDNT* article by Behm goes on after this section on *secular Greek* writers to show how extrabiblical *Jewish* literature (literature that was written in Greek by Greek-speaking Jewish authors) had quite a different meaning for these words. Behm's *TDNT* article says, of the Jewish philosopher Philo, that "what Philo denotes by *metanoeō* or *metanoia* is the OT and Jewish concept of conversion, namely, radical turning to God . . . turning from sin . . . change of nature."[21] He says that the Jewish historian Josephus likes to use these terms "for the concept of religious and moral conversion."[22] In addition, Behm says that in the Jewish Apocrypha and pseudepigrapha,

---

[19] Bing, *Lordship Salvation*, 68, quoting J. Behm, in *TDNT* 4:979.
[20] Ibid., 68n30.
[21] *TDNT*, 4:993.
[22] Ibid., 4:995.

"the predominant sense of *metanoeō* is now 'to convert' and of *metanoia* 'conversion.'"[23] He gives many examples.

Reading further in the *TDNT* article, we reach this section heading: "*metanoeō* and *metanoia* in the New Testament."[24] But Bing does not mention this section, which says, "The terms have religious and ethical significance along the lines of the OT and Jewish concept of conversion, for which there is no analogy in secular Greek. . . . *Metanoeō* and *metanoia* are the forms in which the NT gives new expression to the ancient concept of religious and moral conversion."[25] With reference to passages from Acts, Hebrews, 1 Peter, and Revelation, it says, "It is a turning away from evil . . . and a turning towards God."[26]

This is a very different picture of the *TDNT* article from the one given by Charles Bing, who simply quoted its earlier section on *secular* Greek literature to say that "for the Greeks *metanoeō* never suggests an alteration in the total moral attitude, a profound change in life's direction, a conversion which affects the whole conduct."[27] That is not what the article said about the New Testament use of the term.

In addition to misrepresenting the entry on *metanoeō* in the BAGD lexicon and the article on *metanoeō, metanoia* in *TDNT*, Bing includes the following quotation from A. T. Robertson, a highly regarded expert in New Testament Greek from the early half of the twentieth century. Quoting Robertson's well-known work *Word Pictures in the New Testament*, Bing says this:

---

[23] Ibid., 4:991.
[24] Ibid., 4:999.
[25] Ibid., 4:999–1,000.
[26] Ibid., 4:1,004.
[27] Bing, *Lordship Salvation*, 68, quoting J. Behm, in *TDNT* 4:979.

A. T. Robertson remarked, "It is a linguistic and theological tragedy that we have to go on using 'repentance' for *metanoia*."[28]

This would seem to support Bing's position, because Bing uses this quotation to give documentation to his claim, "It is unfortunate that *metanoeō* is translated 'repent' in the English Bible, for the English etymology denotes more the idea of penitence as sorrow, or worse, the Catholic doctrine of penance, than it does the more accurate 'change of mind.'"[29] But when we consult the two relevant locations in Robertson's *Word Pictures in the New Testament*, we find that Robertson's objection moves in just the opposite direction of what Bing claims. Bing wants the term to mean simply "change of mind" with no nuance of resolve to turn from sin or change one's life. But Robertson's objection is that the English word *repent* can cause people to focus too much on feeling sorry about sin and too little on changing their lives. Robertson says this (commenting on 2 Cor. 7:9):

> Note the sharp difference here between "sorrow" (*lupē*) . . . and "repentance" (*metanoia*) or *change of mind and life*. It is a linguistic and theological tragedy that we have to go on using "repentance" for *metanoia*.

Then, in commenting on the next verse, Robertson says,

> *"Change of mind and life"* [is] shown by *metanoian* (*metanoeō*) and wrongly translated "repentance."[30]

---

[28] Ibid., 69n41, citing 6:241 and 1:24 in Robertson's work.
[29] Ibid., 69.
[30] Archibald T. Robertson, *Word Pictures in the New Testament*, 6 vols. (Grand Rapids, MI: Baker, 1931), 4:240–41; emphasis added.

In the other place that Bing cites from Robertson, we find Robertson's same objection, that in English the word *repent* places too much emphasis on mere sorrow and too little emphasis on change of conduct:

> The trouble is that the English word "repent" means "to be sorry again." . . . John did not call on the people to be sorry, but to change (think afterwards) their mental attitudes (*metanoeite*) *and conduct*.[31]

Therefore the "tragedy" that A. T. Robertson was claiming for the translation "repentance" was that this English word did not place enough emphasis on the need for a change of *both mind and life*. He did not object that the nuance of sorrow or remorse for sin was incorrect but that the commitment to an entire change of life was not represented clearly enough. Bing quotes Robertson to claim support for his proposed meaning "change of mind," but Robertson never argued for these terms to mean a mere "change of mind."

Finally, Bing quotes one other recognized authority when he says, "See supporting comments by Berkhof, *Theology*, 480–481." This reference to Louis Berkhof's widely used *Systematic Theology* is in Bing's footnote supporting the claim that a "more accurate" translation of *metanoia* would be "change of mind."[32] But when we read those pages in Berkhof, we find material far different from Bing's definition "change of mind." Berkhof repeatedly emphasizes that a turning from former sins

---

[31] Ibid., 1:24; emphasis added.
[32] Bing, *Lordship Salvation*, 69n41.

and turning to a new way of life is essential in the meaning of the word:

> Metanoia (verbal form metanoeō). This is the most common word for conversion in the New Testament, and is also the most fundamental of the terms employed. . . . In the English Bible the word is translated "repentance," but this hardly does justice to the original, since it gives undue prominence to the emotional element. . . . In the New Testament . . . it denotes primarily a change of mind, taking a wiser view of the past, including *regret for the ill then done, and leading to a change of life for the better*. . . . While maintaining that the word denotes primarily a change of mind, we should not lose sight of the fact that its meaning is not limited to the intellectual, theoretical consciousness, but also *includes the moral consciousness, the conscience*. . . . Metanoia includes a *conscious opposition to the former condition*. This is an essential element in it, and therefore deserves careful attention. *To be converted*, is not merely to pass from one conscious direction to another, but to do it with *a clearly perceived aversion to the former direction*.[33]

It is surprising, therefore, that Charles Bing says that these pages in Berkhof give "supporting comments" for his understanding of repentance. They, in fact, support the very viewpoint that he denies.

Other reference works also differ with Bing's definition "change of mind" for New Testament usages. The recent *New International Dictionary of New Testament Theology and Ex-*

---

[33] Louis Berkhof, *Systematic Theology* (Grand Rapids, MI: Eerdmans, 1941), 480–81; emphasis added.

egesis says that in later Jewish-Greek writings, "the term has in view the conversion of the whole person." In the Synoptic Gospels, "repentance is viewed in terms of commitment to a person; the call to repentance becomes a call to discipleship." In Acts, "the call for repentance" included a call to "conversion," which is "turning from evil . . . to God."[34]

The older Greek lexicon by J. H. Thayer says that *metanoeō* means "to change one's mind for the better, heartily to amend with abhorrence of one's past sins."[35] The specialized lexicon by Moulton and Milligan, compiled with particular reference to the papyri and other nonliterary sources, says of *metanoeō* that "in the New Testament it is more than 'repent,' and indicates a complete change of attitude, spiritual and moral, towards God."[36] The Greek lexicon by Louw and Nida defines *metanoeō* and *metanoia* as "to change one's way of life as the result of a complete change of attitude with regard to sin and righteousness," and they further explain that in the New Testament the emphasis "seems to be more specifically in the total change, both in thought and behavior, with respect to how one should both think and act."[37]

Bing has an extensive section (70–83) in which he repeatedly attempts to explain various New Testament passages on repentance, arguing that his definition "change of mind" (with-

[34] *New International Dictionary of New Testament Theology and Exegesis*, 5 vols., ed. Moises Silva (Grand Rapids, MI: Zondervan, 2014), 3:291–92.

[35] J. H. Thayer, *A Greek-English Lexicon of the New Testament*, 4th ed. (Edinburgh: T&T Clark, 1901), 405.

[36] James Moulton and George Milligan, *The Vocabulary of the Greek New Testament: Illustrated from the Papyri and Other Non-Literary Sources* (Grand Rapids, MI: Eerdmans, 1930), 404.

[37] Johannes P. Louw and Eugene A. Nida, *A Greek-English Lexicon of the New Testament Based on Semantic Domains*, 2 vols. (New York: United Bible Societies, 1988), 1:510 (sec. 41.52).

out any necessary nuance of sorrow for past sins or resolve to change one's conduct of life) is suitable in each passage, but he repeatedly fails to account for the fact that no standard lexicon or other reference work on the meanings of Greek words in the New Testament supports his understanding of *metanoeō* and *metanoia* in these passages.

B. ALL ENGLISH TRANSLATIONS SAY "REPENT!" AND NOT "CHANGE YOUR MIND!"

There is yet another significant argument against the common Free Grace definition of *repentance* as a mere "change of mind": the definition "change of mind" differs from all widely known English Bible translations.

Take, for example, the first instance of *metanoeō* in the New Testament, which reports John the Baptist preaching and saying, *"Repent,* for the kingdom of heaven is at hand" (Matt. 3:2). This verb is translated as "repent" in the following Bible versions: KJV, NKJV, ESV, NASB, NIV, NET, HCSB, NLT, RSV, and NRSV. I know of no Bible translation that translates this verse as, *"Change your minds,* for the kingdom of heaven is at hand." And for good reason; the English word *repent* does not mean merely "change your mind" but has the following meanings:

> 1. To feel remorse, contrition, or self-reproach for what one has done or failed to do; be contrite. 2. To feel such regret for past conduct as to change one's mind regarding it: *repented of intemperate behavior.* 3. To make a change for the better as a result of remorse or contrition for one's sins.[38]

---

[38] *American Heritage Dictionary,* 4th ed. (Boston: Houghton Mifflin, 2006), s.v. "repent."

Those are three related but slightly distinct meanings for *repent*. Of those three senses, the meaning that would most naturally come to mind for English-speaking readers of the New Testament would be the one connected to "sins," or meaning (3), or perhaps a combined sense of (2) and (3), including making a change for the better, or resolving to make a change for the better, "as a result of remorse or contrition for one's sins." That is the sense that is best suited to the New Testament contexts where English translators have used this word, and that is naturally the sense in which they expected it to be understood.[39]

This is significant. It means that all the verses in the New Testament that use the word *repent* in English are also arguments against the Free Grace position, that *repent* means "to change one's mind." For example:

Repent [not: *Change your mind*], for the kingdom of heaven is at hand. (Matt. 3:2)

From that time Jesus began to preach, saying, "*Repent* [not: *Change your mind*], for the kingdom of heaven is at hand." (Matt. 4:17)

. . . and that *repentance* [not: *a change of mind*] and forgiveness of sins should be proclaimed in his name to all nations, beginning from Jerusalem. (Luke 24:47)

And Peter said to them, "*Repent* [not: *Change your mind*] and be baptized every one of you in the name of Jesus Christ

---

[39] Even meaning (2) by itself, "To feel such regret for past conduct as to change one's mind regarding it: *repented of intemperate behavior*," implies not merely a change of opinion but a change in thinking so that one is resolved no longer to continue that pattern of behavior.

for the forgiveness of your sins, and you will receive the gift of the Holy Spirit." (Acts 2:38)

Repent [not: *Change your mind*] therefore, and turn back, that your sins may be blotted out. (Acts 3:19)

The times of ignorance God overlooked, but now he commands all people everywhere to *repent* [not: *change their minds*]. (Acts 17:30)

[Paul says that he] . . . declared first to those in Damascus, then in Jerusalem and throughout all the region of Judea, and also to the Gentiles, that they should *repent* [not: *change their minds*] and turn to God, performing deeds in keeping with their repentance. (Acts 26:20)

These verses and others like them with the English word *repent* give further evidence that no committee of English Bible translators has agreed with Bing's definition, "change of mind."

2. An optional resolve to turn from sin

A different explanation of repentance is given by other Free Grace advocates. They say that *repentance* means "an internal resolve to turn from one's sins." I find this to be close to my own definition (see p. 42), except that the Free Grace advocates who define it this way then go on to specify that such an internal resolve to turn from sin is *not necessary* before saving faith or as part of saving faith, but is desirable afterward. David R. Anderson holds this view. He writes,

We suggest this meaning: *an internal resolve to turn from one's sins.* We think this meaning will make good sense in every New Testament use.[40]

Immediately after this definition, Anderson adds that such repentance is not a necessary part of saving faith:

> Once again, we ask the question, if repentance is the internal resolve to turn from one's sins, is repentance a condition for receiving eternal life? And once again, we conclude, no.[41]

Then Anderson explains that repentance *is* necessary for enjoying fellowship with God after one becomes a Christian:

> Repentance is not a condition for *receiving* eternal life, but it is a condition for *possessing* eternal life. By possessing eternal life we refer to enjoying a quality of life that only the believer in fellowship with God can have.[42]

Free Grace author Zane Hodges defines repentance in a similar way:

> So far we have reached two fundamental conclusions about repentance. These are: (1) that repentance is not in any way a condition for eternal salvation; and (2) repentance is the

---

[40] David R. Anderson, *Free Grace Soteriology*, ed. James Reitman, rev. ed. (The Woodlands, TX: Grace Theology Press, 2012), 137–38.
[41] Ibid., 138.
[42] Ibid. Anderson's claim that some Christians can *receive* eternal life but not *possess* eternal life is one example of a common Free Grace tendency to create endless specialized subcategories of New Testament terms in order to find some way or other to find a different explanation for New Testament verses that apparently contradict the Free Grace view. (See a statement of amazement and frustration from Tom Schreiner on pp. 138–139).

decision to turn from sin to avoid, or bring to an end, God's temporal judgment.[43]

The problem with this view, and the reason why it seems so unpersuasive, is the very frequent inclusion of "repentance" in several of the most basic summaries of the initial evangelistic message preached by the New Testament apostles. Here is a recap of those passages in light of Anderson's claim that repentance is not required for saving faith.

If repentance were merely optional for salvation, it is unlikely that Jesus would summarize the gospel proclamation to the whole world as only including two things, "that *repentance* and *forgiveness of sins* should be proclaimed in his name to all nations," with the first item only an optional and desirable factor, something not necessary for saving faith (Luke 24:47).

If repentance were merely optional, as Anderson and Hodges claim, it is unlikely to be the first thing that Paul would mention that God commands the Athenian philosophers: "The times of ignorance God overlooked, but now he commands all people everywhere to *repent*" (Acts 17:30). Would Paul actually say this about something which is *optional* and which people will learn about *after* they come to saving faith?

If repentance were merely optional, it is unlikely that Paul would summarize his gospel preaching in Ephesus by saying that he was continually "testifying both to Jews and to Greeks of *repentance toward God* and of faith in our Lord Jesus Christ"

---

[43] Zane Hodges, *Harmony with God: A Fresh Look at Repentance* (Dallas: Redencion Viva, 2001), 57. Robert Wilkin has a similar understanding of repentance: "Both in the Old Testament and in the New Testament repentance is turning from sins. . . . Repentance is turning from one's sins in order to escape temporal judgment." Robert Wilkin, *The Ten Most Misunderstood Words in the Bible* (The Woodlands, TX: Grace Evangelical Society, 2012), 108–9; see also 174.

(Acts 20:21). Would something optional be mentioned before something necessary in such a summary of his gospel message?[44]

If repentance were merely optional, it is unlikely that Paul would summarize to King Agrippa that his gospel message was this: "Therefore, O King Agrippa, I was not disobedient to the heavenly vision, but declared first to those in Damascus, then in Jerusalem and throughout all the region of Judea, and also to the Gentiles, that they should *repent* and turn to God, performing deeds in keeping with their repentance" (Acts 26:19–20). Why would Paul mention something optional that comes after saving faith before he mentions turning to God in initial saving faith?

If repentance were something merely optional or desirable for Christians after they have believed, it is unlikely that the author of Hebrews would include it in the "foundation" and mention it just prior to mentioning faith toward God: "not laying again a foundation of repentance from dead works and of faith toward God" (Heb. 6:1).

And if repentance were merely optional, something that comes later in the Christian life, then it is hard to explain why Jesus seeks repentance from love of money (the rich young ruler), or repentance from living with a man apart from marriage (the woman at the well), or repentance from stealing (Zacchaeus the tax collector), in his very first encounter with people. Why talk about an optional and desirable part of the Christian life that comes after conversion to people who are not yet even saved? Therefore this second Free Grace explanation of repentance, that it is *optional and not necessary for saving*

---

[44] In addition, the grammar links "repentance" and "faith" closely together, suggesting that they are two different parts of the same action (see explanation above, p. 40–41 and n. 4).

faith, seems quite inconsistent with repeated summaries of the gospel message as given in various parts of the New Testament.

In conclusion, there are two understandings of repentance among Free Grace supporters.

1) Many understand *repentance* to mean simply a "change of mind." The weakness of this position is that, for the New Testament, this meaning finds no support in any authoritative Greek lexicon or in any modern English translation, none of which translate the Greek terms *metanoeō* and *metanoia* as "change your mind" for New Testament passages. It is a definition unique to Free Grace supporters, without scholarly support from the academic community or any standard Greek reference works. It also lacks support from any English translation of the Bible.

2) A few Free Grace supporters understand *repentance* to mean "an internal resolve to turn from sin" (a reasonably good definition), but then they separate it from initial saving faith, saying that it can come before saving faith, or after saving faith, or not at all in the life of a Christian. The weakness of this position is that it cannot give a satisfactory explanation for the numerous New Testament verses that tie repentance directly to the initial proclamation of the gospel to unbelievers. Therefore those who support this explanation have to adopt highly unusual, unpersuasive explanations of these verses.

C. However, saving faith does not *include* obedience.

I need to add a word of clarification at this point. While I believe that repentance from sin is a necessary part of saving faith, and while I believe that repentance must include a sincere resolve to turn from one's sins and begin to obey Christ, I do not think it is accurate to say that saving faith therefore must *include* obedience to Christ. I believe that saving faith will *result* in obedience, and saving faith will include a *sincere resolve* to turn from sin and to begin a new pattern of obedience, but *a resolve to turn from sin and begin obedience* is not the same as obedience itself. And we must guard jealously the fact that *faith alone* is what saves us, not faith plus obedience.[45]

No historic Protestant confession says that saving faith *includes* obedience. Although Charles Bing quotes two respected evangelical pastors (John Stott and John MacArthur) who have made statements to this effect,[46] the vast majority of evangelical

---

[45] On a related matter, I am also unwilling to say that initial saving faith requires absolute, total commitment of life, because then I do not think anyone in the world would be saved in this lifetime. Yes, I agree that Jesus demands total commitment of life from us (see Luke 9:23–24; 14:26), but because of our weakness in this lifetime we still fall short of that high standard, and we must trust him for forgiveness even of that failure.

[46] Charles Bing quotes the following sentence from John MacArthur: "Scripture often equates faith with obedience (John 3:36; Romans 1:5; 16:26; 2 Thessalonians 1:8)." MacArthur, *Gospel According to Jesus*, 48; cited by Bing, *Lordship Salvation*, 21 (citing pp. 32–33 in MacArthur's earlier [1988] edition). I think that MacArthur's sentence is unfortunate and claims too much. MacArthur would have been more precise if he had said of those passages, "Scripture often *connects* faith with obedience," for that is all those passages demonstrate. On the same page, Bing also quotes John Stott as saying that "faith includes obedience." Bing's citation is to *Eternity* magazine 10.17, but this is an incorrect reference. The reference should be to *Eternity* 10.9 (September 1959), 17. Again I think that Stott's statement is too strong, and I clearly disagree with it.
Bing also includes quotations from an unpublished teaching syllabus from a single church and from a 1976 article by Kenneth Gentry in a fairly obscure journal (*Baptist Reformation Review* 5 [Spring 1976]: 55), but these are hardly representative of evangelical Protestant theology generally. Gentry later revised and expanded that article into a book: Kenneth Gentry, *Lord of the Saved* (Phillipsburg, NJ: P&R, 1992; repr. Fountain Inn, SC: Victorious House, 2001). In that book he says that "faith is clearly related to obedience" (p. 20), and he says that "James strongly urges that faith will evidence itself in vitality and works (James 2:14–26)," but I could find nowhere in the book where he said that faith *includes* obedience. (Gentry explained in the preface that he had written that earlier article when he was a second-year seminary student, p. *ix*). Therefore it is surprising that Bing quotes the article so frequently, for a 1976 article by a second-year seminary student is hardly representative of the beliefs of recognized leaders or beliefs in evangelical theology.
Fred Chay and John Correia also quote New Testament professor Robert Stein (not a professor of theology) as saying that true faith includes obedience. *The Faith That Saves* (Beaumont, TX: Grace Line, 2008), 18. I do not think that Stein's statement is representative of evangelical scholars generally. Chay and Correia also have an extensive section (pp. 13–39) in which they argue that the Greek term *pisteuō* ("believe") does not include the idea of obedience, and I agree with their conclusion.

authors clearly avoid making such a claim, and I do not think this view is broadly representative of those who reject Free Grace theology. For example, the Westminster Confession of Faith defines faith as "receiving and resting on Christ and his righteousness" (11.1), but it does not say that faith includes obedience.

As for standard texts on systematic theology, when Louis Berkhof explains the volitional element (Latin *fiducia*) of saving faith, he says, "This third element consists in a personal trust in Christ as Saviour and Lord, including a surrender of the soul as guilty and defiled to Christ, and a reception and appropriation of Christ as the source of pardon and of spiritual life,"[47] but he does not say that faith includes obedience. Charles Hodge has an extensive discussion on the nature of faith, but nowhere does he say that faith includes obedience.[48] Millard Erickson says that "the type of faith necessary for salvation involves both believing that and believing in, or assenting to facts and trusting in a person."[49] He says nothing about faith including obedience. Michael Horton says, "Faith produces obedience, but to suggest that faith is obedience is to confuse justification with sanctification."[50] But he does not say that faith includes obedience. J. I. Packer says, "Though we are justified by faith alone, the faith that justifies is never

[47] Berkhof, *Systematic Theology*, 505.

[48] Charles Hodge, *Systematic Theology*, 3 vols. (1871–1873; repr. Grand Rapids, MI: Eerdmans, 1970), 3:41–113.

[49] Millard Erickson, *Christian Theology*, 2nd ed. (Grand Rapids, MI: Baker, 1998), 953. Erickson also helpfully defines repentance as "godly sorrow for one's sin together with a resolution to turn from it" (p. 950).

[50] Michael Horton, "Introduction: Don't Judge a Book by Its Cover," in *Christ the Lord: The Reformation and Lordship Salvation*, ed. Michael Horton (Eugene, OR: Wipf & Stock, 1992), 36.

alone. It produces moral fruit . . . it transforms one's way of living; it begets virtue. This is not only because holiness is commanded, but also because the regenerate heart, of which *fiducia* is the expression, desires holiness and can find full contentment only in seeking it."[51] John Frame says that "true saving faith involves knowledge, belief, and trust in Christ," and he adds that some works will "always accompany true faith,"[52] but he does not say that faith includes obedience. Finally, in my own book *Systematic Theology*, I say, "If we have genuine saving faith, there will be clear results in obedience in our lives,"[53] but nowhere do I say that faith includes obedience.

Therefore, when Free Grace authors claim, as Charles Bing does, that evangelical scholars who disagree with them believe that "faith includes obedience," they are criticizing a straw man. They are criticizing a viewpoint that, to my knowledge, has been held by no major Protestant confession of faith, no influential Protestant systematic theology text, and no evangelical professor of theology.

Robert Wilkin, executive director of the Grace Evangelical Society, also says that those who disagree with Free Grace teachings say that "faith includes works," and that these people define faith as "including" obedience.[54] But rather than documenting this claim by quoting from recognized theology texts and historic Protestant statements of faith (which never say that faith includes obedience), Wilkin simply attributes this

---

[51] J. I. Packer, *Concise Theology* (Leicester, UK: Inter-Varsity Press, 1993), 160.
[52] John Frame, *Systematic Theology* (Phillipsburg, NJ: P&R, 2013), 953–54.
[53] Grudem, *Systematic Theology*, 805.
[54] Wilkin, *Ten Most Misunderstood Words*, 8–9.

view to unnamed "preachers and theologians" or to "radio and TV preachers, pastors, theologians, popular authors, and missionaries,"[55] or even to "most people within Christianity."[56] In another place Wilkin asserts, "For most Calvinists faith is commitment, obedience, and perseverance."[57] But this statement is simply untrue. I am aware of no recognized Calvinist or Reformed theologian who says that faith *is* obedience or that faith *is* perseverance. They will say that saving faith *results* in obedience and that faith *results* in perseverance, but that is something far different from what Wilkin claims.

D. Conclusion: A weakened gospel

My conclusion in this chapter is that the Free Grace movement preaches a weakened gospel because it avoids any call to people to repent of their sins. This is no minor matter, because repentance from sin is such an important part of the gospel in many New Testament summaries and presentations (see above) that it cannot be omitted without grave consequences in the lives of people who hear such a weakened message.

However, I am not willing to say that the Free Grace gospel is a false gospel. That is far too strong a category to apply here, and it calls to mind Paul's extremely strong condemnation in Galatians 1:6–10. I think it is certainly possible to distinguish between a *true gospel* that is presented in an incomplete or weakened form (such as with Free Grace teaching), and a *false gospel* that simply proclaims falsehood rather than truth about Jesus Christ and his work of redemption.

---

[55] Ibid.
[56] Ibid., 171.
[57] Ibid., 19.

The covenant of the Free Grace Alliance says this:

The sole means of receiving the free gift of eternal life is faith in the Lord Jesus Christ, the Son of God, whose substitutionary death on the cross fully satisfied the requirement for our justification.[58]

That statement is a wonderful summary of the New Testament gospel message, and it is inconceivable to me that anyone could read that statement and say that people who believe and advocate those truths are preaching a false gospel. That would just be a slanderous and wrongful accusation.

Another thing that demonstrates that this is not a false gospel is the fact that many people who have heard the gospel proclamation as explained by Free Grace advocates have come to genuine saving faith in Christ. Even though the message of the need for repentance from sins was omitted, every unbeliever who ever comes to Christ comes with a guilty conscience, and comes to ask for forgiveness, and there is often an instinctive awareness of the need to somehow turn from sin, even though that is not made explicit in the gospel presentation. Therefore many such people actually do repent of their sins in their hearts, at least to some extent, and God looks on that heartfelt repentance and sees it as part of genuine faith. Many others start attending a Free Grace church and then repent later, perhaps as they begin reading the Bible, and at that point they first come to genuine saving faith.

Nevertheless, it still seems to me that a deliberate omission

---

[58] Free Grace Alliance website, accessed February 15, 2015, http://www.freegracealliance.com/covenant.htm.

of the need to call people to repent of their sins constitutes a significant departure from New Testament patterns, and such a departure cannot be taught and practiced without significant harmful consequences to the church and to many of the people who hear such a gospel.

3

False Assurance

Free Grace theology gives false assurance of eternal life to many people who profess faith in Christ but then show no evidence in their pattern of life.

A. The result of the weakened Free Grace gospel is many unsaved people.

The weakening of the gospel message that I discussed in the previous chapter should be a major concern for evangelical Christians today. In spite of the fact that some people come to genuine saving faith under Free Grace preaching, I am deeply concerned that such a weakened gospel message, which lacks any call for people to repent from their sins, will result—and has resulted—in many unsaved people who think they are saved. But they are not.

If you ask them if they are sinners in need of salvation, they will agree. If you ask them if they believe that Jesus died to pay the penalty for their sins, they will agree. They heard that teaching in a church one time and decided that they thought it was true. They "changed their minds" about sin and about Christ and about their need for salvation. Intellectually they believed those things to be true facts about history and about themselves, and on this basis some Free Grace pastors and teachers have assured them that they are saved.

But they have never truly repented from their sins. They are still lacking a necessary component of genuine saving faith, according to frequent and repeated New Testament presentations. They still lack genuine repentance, and so they have never had genuine New Testament faith. They are not born again. They are lost because of a weakened gospel message.

Such people often wonder what is wrong with their Christian lives. Why do they not have the joy that they see in Christians around them? Why does the Bible never seem to make much sense? Why is prayer not very meaningful?

Many of these people do not even go to church anymore, but they still think that they are saved, because, if you were to ask them, they would say that they think it is true that they are sinners in need of salvation, and they think it is true that Jesus died to pay for their sins. Therefore some Free Grace advocates have told them that they were already saved. Forever. And that is all they needed to hear. Now they can't be bothered to go near a church. If a Free Grace pastor warns them that they are going to lose heavenly reward, and that they are "not living up to who they truly are," they will just reason that everybody is going to be happy in heaven anyway, so why care? And they persist in their lives of sin. And they are lost.

B. New Testament epistles frequently warn churchgoers that some of them might not be saved.

The remedy for this situation, according to the New Testament, would be to ask churchgoers (and those who claim to be Christians but don't go to church) to examine their lives to see if there has been a genuine change as a result of being born again. Authors of the New Testament epistles repeatedly write to various churches telling them that some patterns of conduct are evidence of being born again, but other patterns of life are inconsistent with the way a born-again Christian will act. They frequently warn people that if there has been no change in their pattern of life, they might not yet be truly saved.

It is important to recognize that these warnings were written not to people outside the church but to people who would be listening to the New Testament epistles as they were read aloud in New Testament churches. The New Testament authors do not hesitate to warn their readers that *some who are among them might not be saved*. I expect that this is an unpopular teaching in many circles today, but I cannot see the New Testament as teaching anything else.

The best-known passage on this subject is James 2, which says that "faith without works is dead":

> What good is it, my brothers, if someone says he has faith but does not have works? Can that faith save him? If a brother or sister is poorly clothed and lacking in daily food, and one of you says to them, "Go in peace, be warmed and filled," without giving them the things needed for the body,

what good is that? So also faith by itself, if it does not have works, is dead. (James 2:14–17)[1]

If a person has no good works, if there is no change in his life, then he has "dead faith"—and verse 14 implies that that kind of faith cannot save a person, because James expects the answer no when he asks the question, "Can that faith save him?"[2]

There are several other passages that likewise address listeners in congregations where these epistles were being read aloud. These additional passages also challenge churchgoing people to be sure that they have genuine, saving faith, not merely superficial intellectual agreement with the facts of the gospel:

Or do you not know that the unrighteous will not inherit the kingdom of God? Do not be deceived: neither the sexually immoral, nor idolaters, nor adulterers, nor men who practice homosexuality, nor thieves, nor the greedy, nor drunkards, nor revilers, nor swindlers will inherit the kingdom of God. And such were some of you. But you were washed, you were sanctified, you were justified in the name of the Lord Jesus Christ and by the Spirit of our God. (1 Cor. 6:9–11; Paul contrasts "the unrighteous" and "the saints" as two different groups in vv. 1–2)

Examine yourselves, to see whether you are in the faith. Test yourselves. Or do you not realize this about yourselves, that

---

[1] I am aware that for every New Testament passage I quote, Free Grace literature will have some alternative explanation, usually an explanation that would not occur to ordinary readers of the Bible. I will discuss some of those explanations below (see chap. 5).

[2] The Greek interrogative particle *mē* at the beginning of the sentence indicates that the author expects a negative answer to the question.

Jesus Christ is in you?—unless indeed you fail to meet the test! (2 Cor. 13:5)

Take care, brothers, lest there be in any of you an evil, unbelieving heart, leading you to fall away from the living God. (Heb. 3:12)

And by this we know that we have come to know him, if we keep his commandments. Whoever says "I know him" but does not keep his commandments is a liar, and the truth is not in him, but whoever keeps his word, in him truly the love of God is perfected. By this we may know that we are in him: whoever says he abides in him ought to walk in the same way in which he walked. (1 John 2:3–6)[3]

No one who abides in him keeps on sinning; no one who keeps on sinning has either seen him or known him. (1 John 3:6)

No one born of God makes a practice of sinning, for God's seed abides in him, and he cannot keep on sinning because

---

[3] Free Grace supporters reply that chapters 1–4 of 1 John give tests of who is in fellowship with God and who is not (see Joseph Dillow, *Final Destiny: The Future Reign of the Servant Kings* [Monument, CO: Paniym Group], 2012), 474–75), rather than tests of whether someone is born again or not. But the verses I have quoted here from 1 John will not bear that interpretation, because coming to "know him" and to be "in him" in 1 John 2:3–6 and 3:6 are descriptions of being born again (see 1 Cor. 1:21; Gal. 4:9; 1 Thess. 4:5; 2 Thess. 1:8; Titus 1:16; 1 John 4:8), not descriptions of some additional level of relationship beyond initial salvation. The other verses cited here distinguish "children of God" from "children of the devil," and talk about knowing that we have "passed out of death into life," both of which are ways of describing what happens at the beginning of the Christian life, not something subsequent to that. The Free Grace claim that chapters 1–4 in 1 John speak of a different category of "fellowship" *rather than* whether a person is born again is built on a false distinction: surely the first requirement for *fellowship* with God is to be born again, and that is why John includes many tests for genuine faith (whether someone is truly born again) throughout the entire epistle. If he wants his readers to have fellowship with him and also "with the Father and with his Son Jesus Christ" (1 John 1:3), then he surely wants to be sure that all of them are born again. Chapters 1–4 of 1 John are not "tests of fellowship" but "requirements for fellowship."

he has been born of God. By this it is evident who are the children of God, and who are the children of the devil: whoever does not practice righteousness is not of God, nor is the one who does not love his brother. (1 John 3:9–10)

We know that we have passed out of death into life, because we love the brothers. Whoever does not love abides in death. (1 John 3:14)

C. The Free Grace view says that people can become complete unbelievers and still be saved.

In contrast to the emphases of the verses cited above, Free Grace advocates do not want to challenge people who *say* they believe in Christ to examine their lives in this way. They claim that we are adding "works" to faith if we say that good works and continuing to believe in Christ are necessary results of saving faith. This leads Zane Hodges to argue, for example, that someone can profess faith in Christ and then later completely deny the Christian faith and become a total unbeliever, yet that person is still saved.[4] Hodges says that when John the Baptist sends a message to Jesus, saying, "Are you the one who is to come, or shall we look for another?" (Luke 7:19), this proves (according to Hodges) that at that point in time, "John the Baptist is not believing. . . . John the Baptist does not believe that Jesus is the Christ, the son of God. . . . But he had not lost the gift of eternal life."[5]

---

[4] Robert Wilkin says that both he and Zane Hodges agree "that once a person believes in Jesus for everlasting life he is eternally secure, even if he later stops believing that (or even if he can never remember believing that)." Robert Wilkin, *The Ten Most Misunderstood Words in the Bible* (The Woodlands, TX: Grace Evangelical Society, 2012), 29n4.

[5] Zane Hodges, *Absolutely Free! A Biblical Reply to Lordship Salvation* (Grand Rapids, MI: Zondervan, 1989), 105–7. However, Luke 3:19 does not prove that John the Baptist had lost all his faith, for his very question implies that he is still looking forward to the Messiah, the "one who is to come," as did all believing Jewish people of his time (see John 1:41;

Hodges also says, "Nowhere does the Word of God guarantee that the believer's faith inevitably will endure. . . . The failure of one's faith is a grim possibility on the field of spiritual battle."[6] A little later he says, "When we trust Him, He guarantees that we possess eternal life (John 6:47)—that we will not come into judgment (John 5:24)—that he will raise us up at the last day (John 6:39–40). And even if we stop believing all this, He remains faithful!"[7]

Joseph Dillow says,

> It is possible for a born-again person to fall away from the faith and cease believing. He is called a carnal Christian and will be subject to severe divine discipline. . . . What he forfeits when he "falls away" is not his eternal destiny but his opportunity to reign with Christ's *Metochoi* [partners] in the coming kingdom.[8]

This refusal of the Free Grace movement to ask people to consider whether they are truly saved—based on continuing in

---

4:25). But because Jesus did not immediately drive out the Roman soldiers and establish an earthly kingdom of God, John was wondering if Jesus was in fact that expected Messiah in whom he hoped and trusted, just as Old Testament saints had done.

[6] Hodges, *Absolutely Free!*, 111. He does not here consider 1 Peter 1:5, where Peter says that Christians are those "who by God's power are being guarded *through faith* for a salvation ready to be revealed in the last time." God's sustaining power works by preserving our faith. I should also make clear at this point that I do not think that a genuine believer can ever lose his or her salvation, for there are many passages in the New Testament that teach that God will protect and keep every genuine believer until the last day (see John 6:38–40; 10:27–29; Rom. 8:1, 30; Eph. 1:13–14; Phil. 1:6; 1 Pet. 1:5; see also Wayne Grudem, *Systematic Theology* [Grand Rapids, MI: Zondervan, 1994], 788–92). But the way that God protects genuine believers is by enabling them to continue to believe; as 1 Peter 1:5 says, we are being guarded "through faith," not apart from our faith. My position is far different from the Free Grace position at this point, for they think that a person can have genuine saving faith and then completely abandon that faith and fall into a state of total unbelief. The implication of that view is that many unbelievers will go to heaven—something the New Testament never teaches!

[7] Hodges, *Absolutely Free!*, 112.

[8] Dillow, *Final Destiny*, 383–85. See my comment on the expression "carnal Christian" (pp. 143–44).

faith and seeing evidence in their good works—is seen in the way they talk about how Christians can gain assurance. For example, the doctrinal statement of the Grace Evangelical Society reads as follows:

> Assurance of everlasting life is based *only* on the promise God makes in His Word that everyone who believes in Jesus Christ alone possesses everlasting life (John 5:24; 1 John 5:9–13). Good works, which can and should follow regeneration, are not necessary for a person to have assurance of everlasting life (Eph. 2:10 ; Titus 3:8).[9]

A similar view of assurance is seen in David Anderson's book *Free Grace Soteriology*, where he advocates giving "absolute assurance" to a brand-new believer:

> We believe a person can have absolute assurance that he is born again the moment he believes. We can give him this assurance, not because of a change in his life that we can feel or see, but because we believe without doubt the promises of God that offer eternal life as a free gift to anyone who believes in Jesus Christ as the son of God and Savior from his sins.[10]

D. Free Grace teaching about assurance makes a fundamental category mistake.

This entire line of argument about assurance involves a fundamental category mistake. All Protestant theologians would

---

[9] Grace Evangelical Society website, accessed February 6, 2015, http://www.faithalone.org/about/beliefs.html; emphasis added.

[10] David R. Anderson, *Free Grace Soteriology*, ed. James Reitman, rev. ed. (The Woodlands, TX: Grace Theology Press, 2012), 220.

agree that our assurance *that Christ's work has earned salvation for sinners* and *that all who trust in Christ will be saved* should be based fully and entirely on the testimony of God in Scripture and what Scripture teaches us about the finished atoning work of Christ. That is how we are to learn about something that has happened outside of us, long before we ever lived: Christ died and paid the penalty for our sins.

But that is not the question here. The question is not:

How do I know that Christ has died for people's sins and that he will save all who believe in him?

The question is, rather:

How do I know *that I have truly believed?*

Reading Bible verses about the atoning work of Christ tells me nothing about whether I have believed or not. Therefore, saying that assurance of my salvation must be based *only* on Scripture and the finished work of Christ is simply a category mistake. It does not address the category of personal belief: How do I know that I *personally have believed?*[11] And here the New Testament gives several verses telling me about various evidences that I have believed, verses that talk about how I can know that I have come to know God, that I am born of God, that I have faith, that I have passed from death to life, and so forth. Such verses include:

---

[11] Zane Hodges refuses to address the question and simply asserts, "People know whether they believe something or not." Rather than explain more deeply what it means to believe in Christ, he dismisses the question as a waste of time: "It is an unproductive waste of time to employ the popular categories—intellect, emotion, or will—as a way of analyzing the mechanics of faith." Hodges, *Absolutely Free!*, 31.

Therefore, brothers, be all the more diligent to confirm your calling and election, for if you practice these qualities [virtue, knowledge, self-control, steadfastness, godliness, brotherly affection, love] you will never fall. (2 Pet. 1:10)

And by this we know that we have come to know him, if we keep his commandments. Whoever says "I know him" but does not keep his commandments is a liar, and the truth is not in him, but whoever keeps his word, in him truly the love of God is perfected. By this we may know that we are in him: whoever says he abides in him ought to walk in the same way in which he walked. (1 John 2:3–6)

We know that we have passed out of death into life, because we love the brothers. Whoever does not love abides in death. (1 John 3:14)

Several other verses show patterns of conduct that are characteristic of unbelievers and characteristic of believers. Here are some of these verses:

Do you not know that the unrighteous will not inherit the kingdom of God? Do not be deceived: neither the sexually immoral, nor idolaters, nor adulterers, nor men who practice homosexuality, nor thieves, nor the greedy, nor drunkards, nor revilers, nor swindlers will inherit the kingdom of God. And such were some of you. But you were washed, you were sanctified, you were justified in the name of the Lord Jesus Christ and by the Spirit of our God. (1 Cor. 6:9–11)

Now the works of the flesh are evident: sexual immorality, impurity, sensuality, idolatry, sorcery, enmity, strife, jealousy, fits of anger, rivalries, dissensions, divisions, envy, drunkenness, orgies, and things like these. I warn you, as I warned you before, that those who do such things will not inherit the kingdom of God. But the fruit of the Spirit is love, joy, peace, patience, kindness, goodness, faithfulness, gentleness, self-control; against such things there is no law. (Gal. 5:19–23)

Do not be deceived: God is not mocked, for whatever one sows, that will he also reap. For the one who sows to his own flesh will from the flesh reap corruption, but the one who sows to the Spirit will from the Spirit reap eternal life. (Gal. 6:7–8)

Sometimes Free Grace supporters will agree that all true believers will have *some* good works in their lives, but they qualify this by saying that for some Christians, there may not be any *evident* works, just works that are known secretly to God. But this response does not really address the question of assurance either, because if the works are not evident, they cannot be used as a basis for assurance that anyone is truly born again. The verses that I have just quoted all speak of evident patterns of conduct, and so they give no basis for saying to someone, "I see no *evident* good works or *evident* change in conduct in your life, but since you professed faith in Christ, you can be sure that you are saved, and therefore you must have some good works that are not evident to anyone."

When Free Grace supporters ask, "Is it not possible that a true believer would fall into a time of disobedience and apparent unbelief?" my reply would be, "Yes, that is certainly possible, but while such a person remains in a state of disobedience and apparent unbelief, we should not give that person unqualified assurance of salvation but should warn that person that he or she does not appear to be saved."

I do not differ with Free Grace supporters over the question of whether a true Christian can fall into a time of disobedience, but over the question of whether, during that time, the person should be assured that he or she will be eternally saved. Prolonged and willful patterns of disobedience and explicit professions of unbelief in Christ give evidence that the person is in fact not saved, as these New Testament verses repeatedly emphasize.[12]

Yet we must also be clear that the historic Protestant position does not make evidence of a changed life the *only* basis for assurance. The internal testimony of the Holy Spirit, who "bears witness with our spirit that we are children of God" (Rom. 8:16), gives another basis for assurance, as does the leading of the Spirit, for "all who are led by the Spirit of God are sons of God" (Rom. 8:14). Another basis for assurance is a deep inner sense of reliance on Jesus Christ for salvation rather than reliance on oneself, for Scripture says, "Whoever believes in the Son has eternal life" (John 3:36), and, "Whoever believes in the Son of God has the testimony in himself" (1 John 5:10;

---

[12] "If we are faithless, he remains faithful—for he cannot deny himself" (2 Tim. 2:13) probably does not refer to complete loss of saving faith but to a temporary weakness of faith or temporary unfaithfulness in conduct, such as Peter's denial of Christ (see discussion in George W. Knight III, *The Pastoral Epistles: A Commentary on the Greek Text*, New International Greek Testament Commentary (Grand Rapids, MI: Eerdmans, 1992), 406–7). The verb *apisteō* need not imply complete unbelief, because one possible meaning is "be unfaithful." See *A Greek-English Lexicon of the New Testament and Other Early Christian Literature*, ed. Walter Bauer, Frederick W. Danker, William Arndt, and F. Wilbur Gingrich (Chicago: University of Chicago Press, 2000), 103.

see also many "whoever believes in him" verses such as John 3:15, 16, 18; 6:35, 47; 7:38; 11:25; Rom. 9:33; 1 Pet. 2:6).

Other verses base assurance on continuing in faith, such as Hebrews 3:14: "We have come to share in Christ, if indeed we hold our original confidence firm to the end"; 1 Peter 1:5: ". . . who by God's power are being guarded *through faith* for a salvation ready to be revealed in the last time"; and Colossians 1:22–23: ". . . in order to present you holy and blameless and above reproach before him, *if indeed you continue in the faith*, stable and steadfast, not shifting from the hope of the gospel that you heard." Still others speak of the fruit of one's life as evidence of salvation; see Matthew 7:15–20: "You will recognize them by their fruits" (see also Gal. 5:22–23 on the fruit of the Spirit).[13]

Such verses genuinely address the question, "How do I know *that I have believed* and that I have been born again?" Verses that speak about the fact that Christ died to pay for people's sins do not address that question. And just dismissing the question, as Hodges does, by saying that "people know whether they believe something or not," does not address the question.

These verses and others mentioned earlier in this chapter (see pp. 86–87) present a composite picture of assurance that comes from *various kinds of evidence in a person's life* (or "fruit"). But the Free Grace view is far different. Joseph Dillow, for example, says that a lack of fruit in a person's life cannot provide a basis for denying the validity of the person's faith:

---

[13] For further discussion of assurance of salvation, see Grudem, *Systematic Theology*, 803–6.

Closely related to the question of faith and knowledge is the question, "How is a saved man to be distinguished from one who professes to be saved but in fact is not?" . . . *We do not discern this by an examination of his fruits* or an assessment of his grief over sin or a measurement of his desire to have fellowship with God. Rather, the presence of a false profession is to be discerned by asking questions that will reveal whether a man understands the gospel and has Christ as the conscious object of faith and whether he believes it. . . . Certainly the lack of fruit in a person's life raises the question, Does he possess the Spirit at all, or if he does, has he quenched Him? But just as the presence of fruit cannot prove whether a person is a Christian, *neither can its absence deny it.*[14]

In order to show that evidence of a change in life should not be used as a basis for assurance, Free Grace advocates sometimes ask, "How many good works does one have to do in order to be assured of salvation?" Or, "How much evidence of a changed life is necessary for assurance?" For example, David Anderson says that if someone has "a list of ways to test your experience to see if you have the necessary proof to be assured of your salvation," that "such tests only stir up doubt, confusion, or self-deception." He goes on to say,

If keeping His commandments is the test, then I must ask:

---

[14] Dillow, *Final Destiny*, 684; emphasis added. According to David Anderson, Free Grace supporters do not say that works have no value at all in assurance, but they say that "works are relegated to a secondary, corroborating role. The only essential ground for the assurance of the believer's salvation is the promises of God" (Anderson, *Free Grace Soteriology*, 216). It is not clear from this statement, however, how works can have a "secondary" role if they cannot be used to prove or disprove a person's salvation. How can works give further assurance if the person already has been given "absolute assurance" (ibid., 220) when he or she first made a profession of faith?

1. How many do I have to keep?
2. How long do I have to keep them?
3. Do I have to keep them perfectly?
4. Are some more important than others?
5. Will He grade on a curve?

The believer quickly becomes disoriented on a sea of subjectivity.[15]

These questions give the impression that Free Grace supporters are looking for something like a mathematical formula by which one can be certain of salvation (How many? How Long?). And when no quantifiable answers are given to these questions, Free Grace advocates claim that, based on a non–Free Grace view, no one could ever have assurance of salvation.[16] Bing writes that "the subjective nature of submission as a requirement for salvation would make assurance unobtainable to the scrutinized life."[17]

But these questions fail to understand how the Bible talks about assurance. It says, "The Spirit himself bears witness with our spirit that we are children of God" (Rom. 8:16), but the testimony of the Holy Spirit can hardly be measured on a numerical scale. It says that one way to "confirm your calling and election" is to supplement your faith with virtue, knowledge, self-control, steadfastness, godliness, brotherly affection, and love (2 Pet. 1:5–10), but it would be impossible to put a numerical value on those qualities in our lives. No numerical measurement can be assigned to walking as Jesus walked (1 John 2:6) or keeping his commandments (1 John 2:3, 4; 3:22, 24; 5:2–3).

---

[15] Anderson, *Free Grace Soteriology*, 216.
[16] See Charles Bing, *Lordship Salvation: A Biblical Evaluation and Response*, 2nd GraceLife ed. (Maitland, FL: Xulon Press, 2010), 179; Anderson, *Free Grace Soteriology*, 216–20.
[17] Bing, *Lordship Salvation*, 179.

Therefore, the proper answer to the question, "How many good works does one have to do in order to be assured of salvation?" is, "Some." To be more specific, *some* change of life gives a basis for *some* measure of assurance, and a greater change of life gives a basis for a stronger assurance. Scripture does not encourage us to demand more specificity than that. A simple diagram might help to clarify the question of assurance (see Diagram 3.1).

Diagram 3.1

Strong evidence of unbelief	Weak evidence of unbelief	Mixed evidence	Weak evidence of belief	Strong evidence of belief
		Unsure about salvation	Weak assurance of salvation	Strong assurance of salvation
Unsaved			Saved	

As Diagram 3.1 indicates, the evidence that a person has actually believed in Christ falls along a spectrum from weak to strong. God alone knows with absolute certainty everyone who is saved and everyone who is lost, for "the Lord knows those who are his" (2 Tim. 2:19), but we can perceive stronger or weaker outward indications of what is actually in someone's heart, both our own hearts and those of others.

In the shaded middle of the spectrum, where people give mixed evidence in their profession of faith and in their conduct of life, we simply have to say that we do not know whether the person is saved or not—the evidence is mixed. One example would be a young man who had understood the gospel clearly and had made a convincing profession of faith in Christ as a teenager but now in his twenties has no affiliation with any Christians or with any church and says he is unsure if he ever really trusted in Christ. But he also gives no strong evidence of unbelief in his personal conduct. A Free Grace supporter would not hesitate to say that this person is clearly saved, based on his earlier profession of faith, but I would say that the New Testament does not allow us to give him any assurance of salvation, for we simply do not have adequate evidence to indicate if he is a believer or not.

If such a person came to me and asked if I thought he was saved, I would say that I don't know but that he should seriously consider some of the warning passages in the New Testament such as, "Take care, brothers, lest there be in any of you an evil, unbelieving heart, leading you to fall away from the living God" (Heb. 3:12); and, "My brothers, if anyone among you wanders from the truth and someone brings him back, let him know that whoever brings back a sinner from his wandering will save his soul from death and will cover a multitude of sins" (James 5:19–20). His failure to seek any affiliation with other Christians also gives reason to soberly consider this verse: "They went out from us, but they were not of us; for if they had been of us, they would have continued with us. But they went out, that it might become plain that they all are not of us" (1 John 2:19). I would tell him that I do not know if he is truly born again or not, but his present pattern of life gives me no reason to give him assurance of salvation.

At the right side of the spectrum, where people give strong evidence of belief by their personal testimony and by the conduct of their lives, they should have strong assurance that they are truly saved, and we should readily encourage them in that assurance.

Finally, I need to make clear that our assurance that Christ has died to pay for our sins, and that all who believe in him will be saved, must be grounded only in the truthfulness of the words of God in Scripture that tell us these things. I am not disagreeing with the Free Grace advocates who say that our assurance *of these things* must be based on the truthfulness of Scripture. I am simply arguing that when they make belief in the truthfulness of Scripture the *only* basis for assurance of my salvation, they make a fundamental category mistake because the truthfulness of Scripture does not answer the other aspect of assurance, the question, "How can I know that I personally have believed these things?" Scripture also tells us how to address that question, in the verses that I mentioned above.

E. The historic Protestant view does not say that assurance of salvation is impossible, but just the opposite.

During my discussions with Free Grace advocates, they have sometimes suggested that people who reject their viewpoint would never be able to gain true assurance of salvation until they die, because who knows whether their lives will take a turn for the worse and they will deny Christ and begin to live a life of sinful rebellion, showing that they were never really saved?

David Anderson says that according to the non–Free Grace position, someone who thinks he is saved has to admit that he might fall away at some time in the future, and this "would prove that [he] never [was a Christian] in the beginning." Therefore, he says, following the logic of the non–Free Grace position, *present* faithfulness is an unreliable basis for present assurance. Only *future* faithfulness can provide any grounds for assurance. But the future is always out there. Until one dies, one can always fall away. Present faithfulness is not firm footing for assurance of salvation.[18]

Robert Wilkin makes similar claims. He says, "If saving faith is more than believing facts, then one cannot have assurance of his eternal destiny by any cognitive method," and, by rejecting his view of saving faith, "it is impossible to be sure of your eternal destiny since you can't be sure that you believe in Christ." If one rejects the Free Grace view, he says, "because no one's life is perfect, certainty of one's eternal destiny is impossible in this system."[19]

But Anderson and Wilkin simply misunderstand the other position when they say that people who reject a Free Grace position are unable to have a confident assurance of their own salvation in this lifetime. The verses I cited above on assurance do not speak that way. Peter tells his hearers "to *confirm* your calling and election" (2 Pet. 1:10), and John says that "if we keep his commandments," then "we *know* that we have come to know him" (1 John 2:3). He also says, "By this we may *know* that we are in him: whoever says he abides in him ought to walk in the same way in which he walked" (1 John 2:5–6).

Therefore, as I wrote over twenty years ago,

No one who has such assurance should wonder, "Will I be able to persevere to the end of my life and therefore be

---

[18] Anderson, *Free Grace Soteriology*, 219–20; emphasis original.
[19] Wilkin, *Ten Most Misunderstood Words*, 13, 16, 19.

saved?" Everyone who gains assurance through such a self-examination should rather think, "I am truly born again; therefore, I will certainly persevere to the end, because I'm being guarded 'by God's power' working through my faith (1 Peter 1:5) and therefore I will never be lost. Jesus will raise me up at the last day and I will enter into his kingdom forever" (John 6:40).[20]

The most influential Protestant tradition since the Reformation, at least in Reformed circles, is represented in the Westminster Confession of Faith (1643–1646), which says:

> Such as truly believe in the Lord Jesus, and love him in sincerity, endeavoring to walk in all good conscience before him, *may, in this life, be certainly assured that they are in the state of grace*. . . . This certainty is not a bare conjectural and probable persuasion . . . but *an infallible assurance of faith* founded upon the *divine truth* of the promises of salvation, the *inward evidences* of those graces unto which these promises are made, the *testimony of the Spirit* of adoption witnessing with our spirits that we are the children of God. (18.1–2)

Therefore, in contrast to the claims of Free Grace advocates, historic Protestantism has taught that believers may attain an "infallible" assurance of salvation and have "certainty" that "they are in the state of grace." This assurance is based on several types of evidence as indicated by many New Testament passages.

---

[20] Grudem, *Systematic Theology*, 805–6. For a longer discussion of the New Testament's teaching on remaining a Christian (or, more precisely, the perseverance of the saints), see the entire chapter, 788–809.

By contrast, the Free Grace movement gives false assurance of eternal life to many unsaved people who have never genuinely repented of their sins, show no evidence of regeneration in their daily lives, and perhaps even profess to be complete unbelievers. The tragic result of this mistaken Free Grace teaching is many people who are unsaved for eternity but who have wrongly been assured that they are saved.

4

Underemphasis on Trust in the Person of Christ

Free Grace teaching overemphasizes agreement with facts and underemphasizes heartfelt trust in the person of Christ.

It is important to recognize that there is a disagreement about the nature of saving faith among different groups in the Free Grace movement. Some Free Grace advocates view faith as *intellectual assent* to the facts of the gospel, while other Free Grace supporters affirm that saving faith must include *trust that is placed in the person of Jesus.* But even this second group underemphasizes the element of trust in the person of Jesus and overemphasizes belief in facts—belief that I am a sinner and belief that Christ has died to pay for my sins.

My argument in this chapter is that the New Testament teaching about saving faith shows that it must go beyond belief that these facts are true (intellectual assent to facts) and must also include heartfelt trust in the living person of Jesus Christ as my Savior and my God forever.

A. Some Free Grace advocates say that faith equals mere intellectual assent.

Representatives of the Free Grace movement who define faith only in terms of agreement with facts (intellectual assent) include Zane Hodges, the founding father of the modern Free Grace movement. Hodges writes,

> Faith . . . is the *inward conviction* that what God says to us in the gospel is true. That—and that alone—is saving faith.[1]

Similarly, the Grace Evangelical Society doctrinal statement says this:

> Faith is the conviction that something is true. To believe in Jesus ("he who believes in Me has everlasting life") is to be convinced that He guarantees everlasting life to all who simply believe in Him for it (John 4:14; 5:24; 6:47; 11:26; 1 Tim. 1:16).

An even more explicit statement of this viewpoint is found in the Free Grace journal, *Grace in Focus*, where Bob Wilkin, executive director of the Grace Evangelical Society, explains:

> Faith in Christ is intellectual assent. Stripped of its pejorative connotation, "intellectual assent" is a good definition of what faith is.[2]

---

[1] Zane Hodges, *Absolutely Free! A Biblical Reply to Lordship Salvation* (Grand Rapids, MI: Zondervan, 1989), 31.
[2] Bob Wilkin, "What Is Free Grace Theology?" *Grace in Focus* 29.5 (September/October, 2014): 27.

Wilkin then gives further explanation as follows:

> For example, do you believe that George Washington was the first President of the United States? If you do, then you know what faith is from a biblical perspective. There is no commitment, no decision of the will, no turning from sins, and no works that are part of faith in Christ. If you are convinced or persuaded that what He promised is true, then you believe in Him.[3]

B. Other Free Grace advocates say that faith includes trust in the person of Christ.

The second Free Grace group disagrees with the first viewpoint and says that faith must rest in the person of Christ, not merely in the truth of propositions about him. This group is best represented by the Free Grace Alliance, whose covenant (doctrinal statement) says this:

> The sole means of receiving the free gift of eternal life is *faith in the Lord Jesus Christ*, the Son of God, whose substitutionary death on the cross fully satisfied the requirement for our justification.[4]

In addition, Charles Bing defines saving faith as trust in Christ:

> What makes saving faith different from any other faith is its object. Therefore, saving faith is defined as trust or confidence in the Lord Jesus Christ as the savior from sin. It is

---

[3] Ibid. On this same page, Wilkin goes on to explain that belief in Jesus's promise of eternal life, in order to constitute valid faith, must not include any idea that works are also necessary.

[4] Free Grace Alliance website, accessed February 8, 2015, http://www.freegracealliance.com /covenant.htm; emphasis added.

personal acceptance of the work of the Lord Jesus Christ on the cross for the sinner.[5]

Some members of the Free Grace Alliance have also affirmed to me in personal correspondence and in private conversation that they do hold to faith in the *person* of Jesus Christ, not merely assent to facts about him. I have also found that to be true in personal interactions with a number of Free Grace supporters. Many wonderful Free Grace Christians whom I know *pray* to Jesus; they don't pray to propositions about Jesus. In church they *worship* Jesus; they don't worship propositions about Jesus. In the language of 1 Peter 1:8, they "love him"; they don't just love propositions about him.

But I still find that that emphasis simply is not there in how they write about the nature of saving faith. It is certainly not there in *Absolutely Free!*, which is the most influential book published by the founding father of today's Free Grace movement, Zane Hodges.[6] In fact, when Hodges discusses Jesus's interaction with Martha in John 11, he gives this reply to his opponents who teach what he calls "lordship salvation":

It is often claimed by those who teach lordship salvation that saving faith cannot be merely "believing facts." But this

---

[5] Charles Bing, *Lordship Salvation: A Biblical Evaluation and Response*, 2nd GraceLife ed. (Maitland, FL: Xulon Press, 2010), 62. He gives a similar definition on pp. 175–76.

[6] See the definition of faith by Zane Hodges, quoted above. On this same page of *Absolutely Free!* Hodges protests, "But is it *mere* intellectual assent? Of course *not*! To describe faith that way is to demean it as a trivial, academic exercise, when in fact it is no such thing" (emphasis original). But then Hodges gives no explanation whatsoever as to how he intends anything more than intellectual assent to the truthfulness of propositions. He says that faith "is the inward conviction that what God says to us in the gospel is true" (p. 31). He explains Abraham's faith by saying, "Abraham trusted God's Word to him—he believed what God said" (p. 32). We look in vain in this entire chapter on faith for any affirmation that includes trust in the person of Jesus that goes beyond mere agreement with statements about him in the Bible.

assertion is both misconceived and clearly wrong. It simply cannot stand up under biblical examination.[7]

He then goes on to explain in detail the importance of believing *facts* about Jesus.[8] Then he says, "By believing the amazing facts about the person of Christ, Martha was trusting Him."[9] In other words, according to Hodges, believing facts about Christ is the same as trusting him.

I recognize that many Free Grace advocates today would differ with Hodges at this point, but a similar emphasis is found in David R. Anderson's book *Free Grace Soteriology*, a book promoted by the Free Grace Alliance. His chapter explaining the nature of faith concludes with a strong emphasis on believing the promises found in Scripture:

> Though saving faith *begins* as an assessment of revealed truth—most notably, God's promises—it is not *consummated* until one *trusts those promises*. One must appropriate those promises for himself and be fully persuaded and *confident in those promises* as his only hope for life eternal. Such faith is not a casual, detached, intellectual process and conclusion. It is an act of trust, whereby one puts the full weight and consequences of his sins on the cross of Christ to open the gates of heaven.[10]

Although Anderson here helpfully emphasizes the fact that

---

[7] Ibid., 37.
[8] Ibid., 37–39.
[9] Ibid., 39.
[10] David R. Anderson, *Free Grace Soteriology*, rev. ed. (The Woodlands, TX: Grace Theology Press, 2012), 184; emphasis added in the third and fourth italicized expressions. On p. 174, he speaks of "trusting in it" (the truth of the gospel). On the other hand, on pp. 175–76 he does speak of "the belief in Jesus which establishes a personal relationship with him."

saving faith involves personal trust and deep confidence, the object of that trust is still said to be the promises of Scripture, not the person of Christ himself. (He does speak of putting the weight of one's sins "on the cross of Christ," but that is still remembering a historical event in the past in distinction from placing trust in the person of Christ as a present, living Savior.)

Joseph Dillow's book *Final Destiny* sometimes explains faith as reliance on Christ and sometimes as persuasion of the truth of biblical evidence. I include here some statements from Dillow's explanation of saving faith:

> Two things differentiate saving faith from mere knowledge. The first may be stated as a persuasion resulting in reliance. Persuasion is deeper than knowledge. Furthermore, persuasion will always result in a degree of *trust in the Object*. . . . It is one thing to intellectually accept certain propositions; it is another to be in a state of reliant trust. It is one thing to believe that God is one, it is another to *believe that* Jesus is God and by *reliance on Him* as one's Savior one can escape the penalty for sin.[11]

> Faith in the Bible . . . is based on a perception of the beauty, glory, and sweetness of divine things as revealed in Scripture and the gospel promise. *The object of biblical faith is the saving work of Christ and the gospel offer.* The evidence on which it rests is the promises of Scripture.[12]

So the evidence from Dillow's statements seems to me to be mixed. In some places, there is an affirmation of trust *in the*

---

[11] Joseph Dillow, *Final Destiny: The Future Reign of the Servant Kings* (Monument, CO: Paniym Group, 2012), 683; emphasis added.
[12] Ibid., 684; emphasis added.

person of Christ as one's Savior, based on the words of Scripture that tell us who Christ is. In other places, it sounds as if believing *facts about Christ* is enough.

I should add, however, that the Grace Evangelical Society and the Free Grace Alliance differ somewhat at this point. The Grace Evangelical Society, under the leadership of Robert Wilkin, repeatedly emphasizes only believing the facts of the gospel (believing that I am a sinner and that Christ died to pay for my sins), with little or no mention of the need to go beyond belief that these facts are true and put one's trust in the person of Jesus Christ. By contrast, the materials promoted by the Free Grace Alliance do affirm in several places that our trust must be placed in the person of Christ, not merely in facts about him.

C. Both groups deemphasize the element of heartfelt trust in the living person of Christ.

Even with these explicit affirmations of the person of Christ as the object of faith, I still do not find in Free Grace literature nearly as much emphasis as we find in the New Testament on *trusting in Christ as a living Savior, coming* to him, *receiving* him, and *believing in him* with one's heart. I will examine several of these passages below.

It does not seem to be accidental that Free Grace literature either explicitly denies that faith is anything more than intellectual assent or else downplays and deemphasizes the element of personal, heartfelt trust in the person of Christ. Such a denial or lack of emphasis would be the natural result of trying to protect the idea that "justification by faith alone" implies that faith should never be said to require repentance from sin or to necessarily result in obedience and good works. It would be the natural result of two considerations:

1) If you emphasize coming into the presence of the person of Christ and trusting him, it becomes very difficult to say that repentance from sin is optional or that subsequent obedience to Christ is optional. The more you talk about the need for trust in the *person* of Christ the more you have to talk about a *personal encounter* with Christ, about coming into his very presence, and that means realizing deeply that he is your God.

To come into the personal presence of Christ is to come before the omnipotent, omniscient, omnipresent, eternal Creator and sustainer of the universe—and he is infinitely pure and holy. The more we emphasize coming into the presence of Christ and trusting him, the more the idea of optional submission to his lordship becomes unthinkable. When we truly realize what it is to come into the majestic presence of the risen Christ, any thought of saying, "Jesus, I'll trust you as my Savior today, and later I might decide to turn from sin and follow you," is as far from our mind as the uttermost part of the sea.

2) Trusting in the person of Christ makes assurance more complex, but Free Grace advocates want to make assurance of salvation simple: if you have believed that you are a sinner and that Christ is your Savior, you can have absolute assurance that you are saved.[13]

On the other hand, if saving faith involves more than just intellectual agreement that some statements in the Bible are true—

---

[13] See, e.g., David Anderson's affirmation: "We believe a person can have absolute assurance that he is born again the moment he believes. We can give him this assurance, not because of a change in his life that we can feel or see, but because we believe without doubt the promises of God that offer eternal life as a free gift to anyone who believes in Jesus Christ as the son of God and Savior from his sins." Anderson, *Free Grace Soteriology*, 220.

if it also includes trusting in Christ as a living person—that is not quite so easy to determine. It opens the question of whether an individual has really trusted in Christ or not. It makes the question of whether a person has genuine faith more complex.

But does the New Testament really teach that saving faith must include personal trust in Christ himself? We can look at several strands of thought in the New Testament that affirm this.

D. Saving faith requires trust in the *person* of Christ, and this means that mental agreement with facts *about* Christ without personal trust in Christ is not saving faith.

In the New Testament, saving faith is regularly represented in terms of an interpersonal interaction between the sinner and Christ, which leads to trust in Christ as a person.

1. Saving faith is pictured as coming to Christ.

"Jesus said to them, 'I am the bread of life; whoever comes to me shall not hunger, and whoever believes in me shall never thirst'" (John 6:35). *Not: whoever agrees with some facts about me shall not hunger.*

"All that the Father gives me will come to me, and whoever comes to me I will never cast out" (John 6:37). *Not: Whoever agrees to some facts about me I will never cast out. To "come to" a person implies interpersonal interaction.*

"No one can come to me unless the Father who sent me draws him. And I will raise him up on the last day" (John 6:44). *Not: No one can agree with some facts about me unless the Father who sent me draws him.*

"On the last day of the feast, the great day, Jesus stood up and cried out, 'If anyone thirsts, let him come to me and drink'" (John 7:37). *Not: If anyone thirsts, let him give mental assent to some facts about me, because "coming to someone" involves personal interaction with the other person, and the image of taking water from him and drinking gives an even stronger indication of personal interaction.*

"Come to me, all who labor and are heavy laden, and I will give you rest. Take my yoke upon you, and learn from me, for I am gentle and lowly in heart, and you will find rest for your souls" (Matt. 11:28–29). *Personal interaction is implied.*

All these passages affirm that trusting in Christ for salvation involves coming into his presence and interacting with him, trusting him personally. A personal encounter is in view.

2. Saving faith is pictured as receiving Christ.

"He came to his own, and his own people did not receive him. But to all who did receive him, who believed in his name, he gave the right to become children of God" (John 1:11–12). *Not: To all who gave mental assent to facts about him* but to all who received him.

In the first-century context, to "receive someone" would have meant welcoming that person into fellowship, into a relationship, probably into one's home, and certainly into one's life. A personal encounter with Jesus Christ is in view. (See also Col. 2:6, "As you received Christ Jesus the Lord, so walk in him.")

3. Saving faith is pictured as believing something in your heart.

> If you confess with your mouth that Jesus is Lord and believe in your heart that God raised him from the dead, you will be saved. For with the heart one believes and is justified, and with the mouth one confesses and is saved. (Rom. 10:9–10)

Paul does not just say "believe in your mind." Belief with one's heart is significant because the heart in Scripture is the center of a person's deepest emotions, beliefs, and convictions, and this includes much more than mere intellectual assent. (Cf. Acts 16:14, which says of Lydia that the Lord "opened her heart"; see also Ezek. 36:26.)

4. Saving faith is portrayed as believing in a person.

Several New Testament verses talk about "believing in" Christ. The most familiar of these is John 3:16:

> For God so loved the world, that he gave his only Son, that whoever *believes in him* should not perish but have eternal life.

The Greek expression here for "believes in" is *pisteuō eis*, where *pisteuō* is the verb for "believe" and *eis* is a preposition meaning "into, in, toward, to." This is notable because, before the time of the New Testament, *pisteuō* was seldom if ever followed by this preposition. It gives a sense of "believing into" Christ, or going out of oneself to place trust in another person. This same preposition (*eis*) is found with *pisteuō* forty-six times in the New Testament (thirty-four of them in John's Gospel). All or nearly all of these verses (along with a few other verses using *pisteuō* with other constructions)[14] take the strong sense indicated in the BDAG lexicon as meaning (2): "to entrust oneself to an entity in complete confidence, believe (in), trust, with implication of total commitment to the one who is trusted."[15] Therefore, over forty verses, such as John 3:16, all containing the strong Greek expression *pisteuō eis* ("believe in"), provide a significant argument that saving faith in the New Testament involves not merely belief in facts in the Bible but placing one's trust in Christ as a person.

To use a simple analogy, an airline passenger can believe that American Airlines has not had a fatal airplane crash in over ten years, with tens of thousands of flights completed successfully, and still experience great fear when he boards the plane. Believing those facts is still different from trusting the pilot himself. But if, when he boards the plane, he sees that the pilot happens to be his neighbor whom he has known

---

[14] I do not claim that *pisteuō* + *eis* is exactly synonymous with *pisteuō* + *en*. There is some overlap in meaning, because *pisteuō* + *en* can sometimes be used in the strong sense of "trust in a person" (at least in John 3:15; similarly, *pisteuō* with no preposition can be used this way: see John 5:24 and Rom. 4:3 with just *pisteuō* + dative). But I have not found that *pisteuō* + *eis* when used of *trusting in a person* ever takes the weakened sense of "believe facts about a person," or "believe the truth of facts reported by the person," without the sense of trust in the person himself.

There are two verses that use *pisteuō* + *eis* but do not specify a person as the object. It seems to me that there is room for disagreement over the meaning of "many believed *in his name*" in John 2:23, but I would take it to refer to genuine trust in Christ, because believing "in his name" is believing in him, in biblical usage. In 1 John 5:10, to believe "in the *witness* that God has borne concerning his Son" is to place confidence in God himself, who speaks this witness, and not to believe this is to make God "a liar," according to this verse.

One other construction, *pisteuō* + *epi*, literally "to believe on" someone (twelve times in the NT) also usually implies a strong sense of movement out of oneself to rest one's trust "on" another person.

[15] *A Greek-English Lexicon of the New Testament and Other Early Christian Literature*, ed. Walter Bauer, Frederick W. Danker, William Arndt, and F. Wilbur Gingrich (Chicago: University of Chicago Press, 2000), 817.

for many years, then he trusts the pilot himself, which is an example of trust in a person.

Similarly, a non-Christian can believe that Jesus died to pay for people's sins but still not trust in the person of Jesus Christ to save him.

I realize, of course, that the verb *pisteuō* sometimes speaks of mere mental assent; words have a range of meanings. We determine the specific meaning within that range from the specific grammatical construction in which the word occurs and from the larger context in which the statement occurs. The BDAG lexicon recognizes this with *pisteuō*, because it gives this as meaning (1): "to consider something to be true and therefore worthy of one's trust."[16]

Yet the fact remains that dozens of verses in the New Testament, especially the many verses with *pisteuō eis*, speak about trust in Christ as a person, "believing in him." Here are some other examples:

> Whoever *believes in him* is not condemned, but whoever does not believe is condemned already, because he has not believed in the name of the only Son of God. (John 3:18)

> Jesus said to them, "I am the bread of life; whoever comes to me shall not hunger, and whoever *believes in me* shall never thirst." (John 6:35)

> For this is the will of my Father, that everyone who looks on the Son and *believes in him* should have eternal life, and I will raise him up on the last day. (John 6:40)

---

[16] Ibid., 816. Examples of the meaning "to consider something to be true" include Matt. 21:32 (believing John the Baptist) and Acts 8:12 (believing Philip).

> Jesus said to her, "I am the resurrection and the life. Whoever *believes in me*, though he die, yet shall he live, and everyone who lives and *believes in me* shall never die." (John 11:25–26)[17]

Therefore, the evidence from several strands of New Testament teaching (verses about coming to Christ, receiving Christ, believing in one's heart, and believing in Christ) all indicate that saving faith requires trust *in the person of Christ*, and that mere mental agreement with facts about Christ is not genuine saving faith.

But if this is true, it gives me deep concern, because the result of a weakened Free Grace gospel will be many unsaved churchgoers who think they are saved but are not. They have never truly received Christ or trusted in him as a person. While they think that they are saved, they are lost.

E. Free Grace misunderstandings of B. B. Warfield on the need to decide to trust in Christ personally

Although all the verses in the previous section emphasize the need to make *a conscious decision to come to Christ and trust him personally*, Free Grace authors such as Joseph Dillow and

---

[17] Remarkably, Joseph Dillow quotes Rudolph Bultmann, the most famous and influential twentieth-century proponent of "demythologizing" the New Testament, to support the idea that "adding prepositions to the word 'faith' like 'believe into,' or 'believe in,' do not change the fundamental meaning. These constructions mean the same thing as 'believe that.'" Dillow, *Final Destiny*, 681, with reference to Bultmann's article on *pisteuō* ("faith") in *Theological Dictionary of the New Testament*, 10 vols., ed. G. Kittel and G. Friedrich, trans. Geoffrey W. Bromiley (Grand Rapids, MI: Eerdmans, 1964–1976), 6:203.

Dillow shows no awareness of the fact that Bultmann's entire approach was to apply a radical skepticism to every supernatural event in the New Testament, thus "demythologizing" the New Testament entirely (that is, draining it of its supernatural elements). Of course Bultmann would want to remove any supernatural elements (such as the idea of *trusting in* the person of Christ, whom we cannot now see) from the New Testament. But he is hardly a reliable guide to understanding the nature of faith in the Bible.

David Anderson deny that such a decision of the will is necessary for saving faith. They base much of their argument on some quotations from famed Princeton theologian B. B. Warfield (1831–1921), but I do not think that Dillow or Anderson have represented Warfield accurately.

In Dillow's book *Final Destiny*, he attempts to give evidence for his claim that "saving faith is simply *believing something is true* and resting confidently in the object of faith. It involves knowledge about the object and then belief and acceptance of that knowledge as valid."[18] Dillow claims that "the will in itself does not seem to be involved in the production of faith."[19] As support for his view that faith just "happens" when a person sees the evidence clearly and does not involve the will, Dillow quotes B. B. Warfield:

> Warfield eliminates a role for the will in producing faith when he says: "Belief . . . is a mental recognition of what is before the mind, as objectively true and real. . . . It is, therefore, impossible that belief should be the product of a volition."[20]

But Dillow fails to tell the reader that that is not Warfield's conclusion about the nature of faith, nor is it even Warfield's definition of what he calls "religious faith." A closer reading of that entire article by Warfield argues directly against the point that Dillow is trying to establish.[21] (Warfield's article, under-

---

[18] Ibid., 679.

[19] Ibid., 680.

[20] Ibid., 680–81, quoting Warfield's article, "Faith in Its Psychological Aspects."

[21] The Warfield essay that Dillow quoted is available in a different edition with different pagination. I found it in B. B. Warfield, "On Faith in Its Psychological Aspects," in *Studies in Theology*, vol. 9, *The Works of Benjamin B. Warfield* (repr. Grand Rapids, MI: Baker, 1991), 315.

stood in its entirety, also argues against David Anderson, who uses the same quotation from Warfield to argue the same point: that "the will has nothing to do with faith at all."[22])

In the statement that Dillow quotes (above), Warfield is not denying that saving faith in Christ must include an element of personal trust (*fiducia*), for he explicitly affirms this very clearly on pages 340–41 of the same article (see below). Rather, in this section, he is beginning a long argument against the idea that faith can exist apart from persuasion of the truth of evidence. He is arguing against the idea that someone can simply "decide" to believe even though there is not adequate evidence on which to base a belief. That is why he says that it is impossible "that belief should be the *product* of a volition." He is arguing that belief must be based on evidence, not on an arbitrary act of the will in the absence of evidence.

This is evident two pages later when Warfield begins a paragraph by saying, "It would seem to be fairly clear that 'belief' is always the product of evidence and that it cannot be created by volitions, whether singly or in any number of repetitions. . . . [It must be] determined by evidence, not by volition."[23]

But in the entire structure of the article, after a long discussion demonstrating that belief must be based on adequate evidence (to which I and all Protestant theologians would agree), he then goes on to a section in the article in which he talks about "What we call religious faith."[24] (Neither Dillow nor Anderson mentions this section on religious faith.) Warfield says

---

[22] Anderson, *Free Grace Soteriology*, 169, uses the same quotation from Warfield.
[23] Warfield, "On Faith," 317.
[24] Ibid., 331.

that when we begin to talk about religious faith, the element of "trust" becomes prominent:

> In what we call religious faith this prominent implication of trust reaches its height. . . . What is prominent in this state of mind is precisely trust. Trust is the active expression of that sense of dependence in which religion largely consists, and it is its presence in these acts of faith, belief, which communicates to them their religious quality *and raises them from mere beliefs of propositions,* the contents of which happen to be of religious purport, to acts possessed of religious character. It is the nature of trust to seek a *personal object* on which to repose, and it is only natural, therefore, that what we call *religious faith does not reach its height in assent to propositions of whatever religious content* and however well fitted to call out religious trust, but *comes to its rights only when it rests with adoring trust on a person.* . . . It rests on the person of God our benefactor, or of Christ our Savior. . . . Faith in God, and above all, faith in Jesus Christ, is just trusting Him in its purity.[25]

In the remaining sections of the article, Warfield affirms several times that saving faith goes beyond believing facts about Christ and must include personally entrusting oneself to him. Following are some further statements.

> [The expression] "to believe in," "to have faith in" comes to mean simply "entrust yourself to."[26]

---

[25] Ibid., 331–32; emphasis added.
[26] Ibid., 332.

The sinful heart—which is enmity towards God—is incapable of that supreme act of trust in God—or rather of entrusting itself to God its Saviour—which itself has absorbed into itself the term "faith" in its Christian connotation.[27]

[Faith comes to terminate] ultimately on God Himself and to rest on Him for our works. And thus it manifests its fundamental and universal character as trust in God . . . as the inexhaustible fountain to his creatures of all blessedness.[28]

The Protestant theologians have generally explained that faith includes in itself the three elements of *notitia, assensus, fiducia*. Their primary object has been, no doubt, to protest against the Romish [i.e., Roman Catholic] conception which limits faith to the assent of the understanding. *The stress of the Protestant definition lies therefore upon the fiducial element.* This stress has not led the Protestant theologians generally, however, to eliminate from the conception of faith the elements of understanding and assent.[29]

Speaking broadly, Protestant theologians have reckoned all these elements as embraced within the mental movement we call faith itself; and they have obviously been right in so doing. . . . No true faith has arisen unless there has been a perception of the object to be believed or believed in, an assent to its worthiness to be believed or believed in, and *a commitment of ourselves to it as true and trustworthy.* We cannot be said to believe or trust in a thing or a person of which we have no knowledge.[30]

---

[27] Ibid., 337.
[28] Ibid., 340.
[29] Ibid., 340–41; emphasis added.
[30] Ibid., 341; emphasis added.

In every movement of faith, therefore, from the lowest to
the highest, there is an intellectual, and emotional, *and a
voluntary* element.[31]

In another article, Warfield explains that faith is "'an absolute transference of trust from ourselves to another,' a complete self-surrender to Christ."[32] A little later in the same article
Warfield explains that faith "obviously contains in it, therefore,
an element of knowledge . . . and it as obviously issues in conduct. . . . But *it consists neither in assent nor in obedience,* but
in a reliant trust in the invisible Author of all good. . . . [It] is
not a mere belief in God's existence and justice and goodness,
or crediting of His word and promises, but a practical counting
of Him faithful." Faith *"is thus the going out of the heart from
itself and its resting on God in confident trust for all good."*[33]

So Warfield repeatedly expresses an understanding of faith
by which it includes more than agreement with the facts that I
am a sinner and that Jesus died and paid for my sins. He says
that Protestant theologians generally, and rightly, have seen
saving faith as including a strong voluntary element of personal
trust in Christ, resting on him, entrusting one's life to him. This
emphasis is different from what Dillow and Anderson represent
Warfield as saying.

Therefore it appears that there is a troubling pattern of
teaching (at least among some prominent voices in the Free

---

[31] Ibid.; emphasis added.
[32] B. B. Warfield, "The Biblical Doctrine of Faith," in *Biblical Doctrines*, vol. 2, 478.
Richard A. Muller says that orthodox theologians following the Reformation did not
"equate faith with assent to doctrinal propositions elicited from the biblical text" but
taught that saving faith "embraces the whole person and is both intellectual and volitional"
(Richard A. Muller, *Post-Reformation Reformed Dogmatics*, 4 vols., 2nd ed. (Grand
Rapids, MI: Baker, 2003), 2:290–91.
[33] Warfield, "Biblical Doctrine of Faith," 501–2; emphasis added.

Grace movement) that almost exclusively emphasizes belief in facts about Christ and repeatedly downplays or even denies the very heart of saving faith in the New Testament—a conscious decision of the will to "come to him" in personal encounter and "receive him" and "believe in him" as a living person, as the one who promises us, "Whoever comes to me I will never cast out" (John 6:37).

But if there is such a failure to emphasize trust in Christ as a person in Free Grace churches, there is also a danger that many who attend Free Grace churches have given intellectual assent to all the right doctrines but have never come to trust in the actual person of Christ for their salvation. And if they have never trusted in the person of Christ, they do not have genuine saving faith as the New Testament defines it.

Unlikely Interpretations

Free Grace advocates have to adopt numerous highly unlikely interpretations of the New Testament because of the need to defend their mistaken understanding of the word "alone" in the phrase "faith alone."

Regarding the Bible passages we have considered up to this point, I realize that Free Grace supporters have developed specialized explanations that enable them to put these verses into various special categories *other than* those pertaining to initial saving faith or evidence of saving faith.

It is not my purpose to interact with all of those explanations in detail at this point, except to say that I think Free Grace "insiders" have no idea how strained, how idiosyncratic, how artificial and contrived, how insensitive to context, and how completely unpersuasive and foreign to the New Testament these explanations sound. Again and again they bear the marks of special pleading. In some cases, they are not even mentioned as legitimate exegetical alternatives in the standard commentaries because no serious interpreter in history of the church has held these interpretations.

A. Some examples of unlikely interpretations

To get an idea of the unusual nature of these Free Grace interpretations, consider the following explanations from the most influential Free Grace book, written by the most influential promoter of the Free Grace viewpoint, Zane Hodges:[1]

1. Luke 16:30

In Jesus's parable, after the rich man had died and gone to hell, he expressed concern for his brothers who were still alive, as follows:

> And he said, "No, father Abraham, but if someone goes to them from the dead, they will *repent*."

Hodges is not willing to say that repentance is necessary for salvation, but this verse provides a difficulty for his view, because it implies that the brothers need to repent in order to be saved. Hodges's solution is that this verse teaches incorrect doctrine: "We are certainly not to infer that he awakened in hell with a clear-cut theology of salvation by grace through faith!"[2]

But that understanding of the verse is certainly wrong, for in the next verse Jesus himself assumes that the brothers need

---

[1] I recognize that not all Free Grace supporters will adopt all of these interpretations.

[2] Zane Hodges, *Absolutely Free! A Biblical Reply to Lordship Salvation* (Grand Rapids, MI: Zondervan, 1989), 226.

repentance, when he has Abraham say that they would not even be convinced "if someone should rise from the dead" (Luke 16:31). Jesus's argument about their culpability would not be persuasive unless the reader assumes that they needed to be "convinced" of the thing that has just been mentioned, the need to repent.

2. John 15:1–2

Jesus said, "I am the true vine, and my Father is the vine-dresser. *Every branch in me that does not bear fruit he takes away*, and every branch that does bear fruit he prunes, that it may bear more fruit."

This passage creates a difficulty for the Free Grace position because it shows that if someone's life is unfruitful, that person will be taken away from Christ, who is the true vine.[3] To avoid this difficulty, Free Grace supporters argue that "takes away" should instead be translated "he lifts up" (another possible meaning of the Greek verb *airō*), so that the branches may get more sunlight and become fruitful. They say the verse means, "Every branch in me that does not bear fruit he *lifts up*." For support, they refer to sources that say that grapevines were supported on wooden poles or trellises in the ancient world.[4]

However, when I consulted the Bible dictionaries and other reference works on ancient viticulture (raising vines) that Bing

---

[3] This passage does not teach that true believers can lose their salvation, for "every branch in me" could well imply just a loose connection such as association with a church, and not genuine salvation.

[4] See Charles Bing, *Lordship Salvation: A Biblical Evaluation and Response*, 2nd GraceLife ed. (Maitland, FL: Xulon Press, 2010), 41–42; Joseph Dillow, *Final Destiny: The Future Reign of the Servant Kings* (Monument, CO: Paniym Group, 2012), 608–10. Both authors refer to reference works dealing with viticulture in ancient Palestine.

and Dillow cited, though there was evidence that grapevines were sometimes supported on wooden posts or frames (which no one denies), there was no evidence given by any source showing that unfruitful vines or branches were "lifted up" so that they would bear more fruit. No Free Grace publication that I could find produced any evidence from the ancient world that said that unfruitful vines or branches were "lifted up."[5] This means that the unusual Free Grace interpretation of this passage is a purely speculative argument with no supporting evidence.

Moreover, this position does not fit the wording of the verse. The only kind of branch that the Father does anything to "that it may bear more fruit" is the branch "that *does* bear fruit." Even if we try the meaning "lifts up" in the verse, the verse does not say, "Every branch in me that does not bear fruit he *lifts up that it may bear more fruit*," nor does it say, "that *they* [plural, meaning both kinds of branches] may bear more fruit." It says only that the fruitful branch is pruned "that *it* may bear more fruit."

The most extensive description that I found of ancient agricultural methods with regard to grapevines is the discussion in *Natural History* by Pliny the Elder (AD 23–79, very close to the

---

[5] However, one reference work mentioned by Bing was Ralph Gower, *The New Manners and Customs of Bible Times* (Chicago: Moody, 1987), 106. But on that page Gower says that "pruning was done . . . to get rid of weak, broken, or diseased branches so that the vine would produce the best possible grapes." This is the opposite of saying that branches that do not bear fruit are "lifted up" so that they would bear more fruit.

Another reference work that Bing cites is A. C. Schultz, "Vine, vineyard," in *Zondervan Pictorial Encyclopedia of the Bible*, 5 vols., ed. Merrill Tenney (Grand Rapids, MI: Zondervan, 1975), 5:882–84, and Bing gives this reference to support his claim that "many cite Palestinian practice in viticulture to confirm" his claim that "the vinedresser is seen lifting the blossoming grape branches off the ground so that they will be more exposed to the sun and less susceptible to damage, and thus become fruitful." But Schultz says nothing of the kind, but rather says that "most of the vines in Palestine trail on the ground, because it is believed that the grapes ripen more slowly under the shadow of the leaves. Too much exposure to the sun in the early period of the growth of the clusters would cause the grapes to ripen before they were fully grown" (p. 882). If anything, this statement proves the opposite of what Bing says it does.

time of Jesus's earthly ministry). He includes some instructions that are relevant for understanding John 15, for they show that unfruitful vines are to be cut off and burned:

> If a vine is making poor growth, make a bonfire of its shoots and plow in the ashes therefrom.[6]

> If a meager vine has not got suitable branches, it is a very good plan to cut it back to the ground and get it to put out new branches.[7]

> . . . pruning away only the decayed parts of the vine and those beginning to wither, and leaving the rest to bear grapes relieved of superfluous weight.[8]

Pliny thus says the opposite of what Free Grace supporters argue. Far from being "lifted up," he says unfruitful branches were cut off and unfruitful vines were burned up in a "bonfire."

3. John 15:6

Here Jesus says,

> If anyone does not abide in me he is thrown away like a branch and withers; and the branches are gathered, thrown into the fire, and burned.

This passage continues Jesus's same teaching about vine and branches, and it is a problem for the Free Grace position because it teaches that people who forsake any relationship with Christ will be "thrown into the fire, and burned," which seems to be a picture of final judgment.

---

[6] Pliny, *Natural History*, 17.6.55 (Loeb Classical Library, vol. 5, 38–39), quoting Cato.
[7] Ibid., 17.35.193 (Loeb Classical Library, 134–35).
[8] Ibid., 17.35.213 (Loeb Classical Library, 148–49).

To get around this problem, Hodges says that this passage is not about salvation but about discipleship and discipline. The branches that are burned are true Christians who are saved, but they will be "cast into the 'fire' of trial and divine chastisement." This is "an experience of spiritual education," not a picture of divine judgment.[9]

But Hodges overlooks the fact that all the biblical examples of burning of vegetation (whether branches, thorns, chaff, or weeds) show that the vegetation is totally burned up. While metal may be purified by fire, there are no examples in Scripture of plant material or wood being *purified* by fire. On the other hand, there are several clear examples of vegetation or plant material being totally destroyed or consumed by fire, as in Matthew 13:40: "Just as the weeds are gathered and burned with fire, so will it be at the end of the age" (see also Matt. 3:12; 2 Sam. 23:6–7; Isa. 9:18; other examples are Lev. 6:12; 13:52, 57; Deut. 7:5; 12:3; Josh. 11:6; Jer. 4:2, 22; Ezek. 15:4–6; 19:12).

4. Acts 11:18

Here we read,

> When they heard these things they fell silent. And they glorified God, saying, "Then to the Gentiles also God has granted repentance that leads to life."

This is the story of Christians in Jerusalem who were at first critical that Peter had preached the gospel to the Gentiles

---

[9] Hodges, *Absolutely Free!*, 137. Bing (*Lordship Salvation*, 40) says that the burning of the branches represents a testing of works for heavenly reward. Dillow (*Final Destiny*, 610–13) says that it represents divine discipline, but not final judgment.

in Cornelius's household. But when Peter told the story of how the Holy Spirit had fallen on them as he preached, and how the members of Cornelius's household had received baptism, their criticism changed to an attitude of amazement and thanksgiving that salvation was also coming even to Gentiles! They were thankful that "to the Gentiles also God has granted repentance that leads to life" (Acts 11:18).

The Free Grace position denies that repentance is essential to saving faith, and therefore Zane Hodges is unwilling to admit that people become Christians through "repentance that leads to life." He has an alternative explanation: "repentance that leads to life" is not the same as "repentance unto eternal life." He says, "Let these words not be misread. Emphatically they do *not* say, 'repentance unto *eternal* life.'"[10]

But here Hodges overlooks the entire structure of the book of Acts. Jesus had predicted that his disciples would be his witnesses "in Jerusalem and in all Judea and Samaria, and to the end of the earth" (Acts 1:8). Peter's preaching of the gospel to the Gentile household of Cornelius in Acts 10 marks the beginning of the remarkable fulfillment of this final stage in the spread of the gospel, which in the previous nine chapters had been proclaimed "in Jerusalem and all Judea and Samaria," but now in chapter 10 is beginning to spread "to the end of the earth."

The Jerusalem Christians were not rejoicing that Gentiles had repented unto some *additional* level of fellowship or discipleship after salvation (as Hodges would have it), but that they had repented at the initial gospel message. Peter was not preaching to Cornelius about advanced discipleship training for

---

[10] Hodges, *Absolutely Free!*, 153; emphasis original.

Christian believers but was fulfilling the prediction of the angel who told Cornelius that Peter "will declare to you a message *by which you will be saved*, you and all your household" (Acts 11:14). Hodges here demonstrates a remarkable evasiveness from the plain force of the text.

5. Acts 17:30

The apostle Paul said,

> The times of ignorance God overlooked, but now he commands all people everywhere to repent.

This is in Paul's first and only recorded message to the Greek philosophers on the Areopagus in Athens.

Acts 17:30 poses a difficulty for Hodges, because the Free Grace view claims that repentance is not necessary for initial saving faith. But here Paul is telling pagan Greek philosophers that God commands them to repent. Hodges's answer is that this verse is not a part of the call to initial saving faith but is something different, a "call to enter into harmonious relations with God"[11] (which would come after saving faith, in Hodges's view).

But Hodges fails to adequately take into account the fact that this passage in Acts 17 is a summary of Paul's initial gospel proclamation to the philosophers in Athens. And in this initial gospel message, the one and only thing he says that God commands is that they repent. In such a context, this wording cannot be anything other than the heart of his gospel message. This call to repent is best understood as Paul's explanation of the only way to escape the judgment that he warns of in the

---

[11] Ibid., 145.

second half of the same sentence: God "commands all people everywhere to repent, *because he has fixed a day on which he will judge the world in righteousness* by a man whom he has appointed; and of this he has given assurance to all by raising him from the dead" (Acts 17:30–31). Repentance, in Paul's preaching, is necessary to escape final judgment, and where genuine repentance is present, saving faith will also be present.

6. Acts 26:19–20

Paul declared,

> Therefore, O King Agrippa, I was not disobedient to the heavenly vision, but declared first to those in Damascus, then in Jerusalem and throughout all the region of Judea, and also to the Gentiles, that they should repent and turn to God, performing deeds in keeping with their repentance.

This is Paul's summary, when he was on trial before King Agrippa, of his entire preaching ministry both to Jews and to Gentiles. He is also no doubt deeply aware that this is an opportunity to call King Agrippa himself to saving faith and that the way he summarizes his gospel message to others will likely be understood by King Agrippa as what Paul is also hoping that Agrippa himself will do: "*repent* and turn to God."

But once again the Free Grace position will not allow repentance to be a necessary part of the initial gospel message. Therefore another explanation for this verse is needed. Hodges's explanation is that here Paul is not summarizing his *initial* gospel message to unbelievers but is explaining how to live a life of holiness and good works *after* one is saved: "'I preach holiness,' Paul is saying. 'I preach the kind of religious experience that turns people to God and produces good works.' . . . Paul is not saying . . . that one cannot be saved without repentance."[12]

However, it is unlikely that Paul would mention an optional call to post-conversion holiness in his summary of what God wanted unsaved Jews and Greeks (and King Agrippa) to do. It is much more likely that this is a summary of the initial things that an unsaved person needs to do in order to be saved: repent and turn to God. In addition, Hodges fails to account for the fact that Paul mentions repentance before he mentions turning to God: "that they should *repent* and *turn to God*." Hodges's interpretation does not make sense, for it would have Paul saying that his ministry was one of declaring to Jews and to Gentiles "that they should *lead a life of holiness* and turn to God." That order of wording would put good works *before* initial saving faith, which Paul certainly would not do.

I agree that the next phrase in Acts 26:20, "performing deeds in keeping with their repentance," describes what will happen after initial saving faith, but that makes sense in the sequence of these things as Paul mentions them: first repentance, then turning to God (which together comprise initial saving faith), then good works, which will follow.

7. Romans 10:9–13

In his epistle to the Romans Paul writes,

> If you confess with your mouth that Jesus is Lord and believe in your heart that God raised him from the dead, *you*

---

[12] Ibid., 163.

will be saved. For with the heart one believes and is justified, and with the mouth one confesses and is saved. For
the Scripture says, "Everyone who believes in him will not
be put to shame." For there is no distinction between Jew
and Greek; for the same Lord is Lord of all, bestowing his
riches on all who call on him. For *"everyone who calls on
the name of the Lord will be saved."*

Zane Hodges says that in this passage, calling on the name
of the Lord to be saved (v. 13) does not mean calling out to
gain eternal salvation but calling out "to obtain His aid and
deliverance in daily life."[13] But Hodges overlooks the fact that
this entire chapter is about Paul's "heart's desire and prayer"
for the Jewish people "that they may be *saved*" (Rom. 10:1),
and this salvation means that Jewish people would have to leave
their present situation of "being ignorant of the righteousness
of God" (v. 3), and obtaining instead "the righteousness based
on faith" (v. 6), which can happen only if they trust in Christ,
who is "the end of the law for righteousness to everyone who
believes" (v. 4). This is a continuation of Paul's heartfelt desire
for his Jewish kinsmen who have rejected Jesus as their Messiah to be saved, a theme that began in 9:1 and is continued
throughout chapters 9, 10, and 11. The repeated theme of
chapters 9–11 is Paul's longing for the Jewish people to obtain

---

[13] Ibid., 196; see all of 194–97; also Dillow, *Final Destiny*, 185–96. Hodges and Dillow
both appeal to other passages where "calling on the name of the Lord" is something done
by Christians. But the thing requested in "calling on the name of the Lord" is specified in
every case by the context, and here the context clearly specifies eternal salvation. Hodges
and Dillow are simply making an exegetical mistake when they import an item that is called
for in *other* passages into this passage. Free Grace advocates Fred Chay and John Correia
say that vv. 9–10 "deal with sanctification" and that this passage "does not intend to say
anything about what we typically referred to as 'salvation.'" Fred Chay and John Correia,
The Faith That Saves (Dallas: Grace Line, 2008), 110.

righteousness through faith in Christ (see 9:30–32), not "to obtain His aid and deliverance in daily life."

This theme of eternal salvation is surely in view in Romans 10:9: "If you confess with your mouth that Jesus is Lord and believe in your heart that God raised him from the dead, you will be *saved*." That is also the meaning of "saved" in verse 13: "Everyone who calls on the name of the Lord will be *saved*." Eternal salvation of the Jewish people is Paul's entire concern in this chapter, and the context gives no hint of discussing "deliverance" from dangers in everyday life.[14]

When Paul mentions the need to both "confess with your mouth" and "believe in your heart," he is not adding to faith another requirement of verbal confession, but, as Leon Morris says, "we should understand them to be closely related as the outward and inward aspects of the same thing. . . . Paul does not contemplate an inner state that is not reflected in outward conduct. If anyone really believes he will confess Christ, so it is natural to link the two."[15]

8. 2 Corinthians 13:5

To the Corinthians Paul writes,

---

[14] Robert Wilkin has another unlikely explanation. He says that "saved" in Romans 10:13 means "saved from Gentile armies." He explains that this passage "refers to Jewish believers at the end of the Tribulation who will call out to Jesus to save them from the Gentile armies that have surrounded Jerusalem." Robert Wilkin, *The Ten Most Misunderstood Words in the Bible* (The Woodlands, TX: Grace Evangelical Society, 2012), 35.

[15] Leon Morris, *The Epistle to the Romans*, Pillar New Testament Commentary (Grand Rapids, MI: Eerdmans, 1988), 384. Similarly, see Douglas Moo, *The Epistle to the Romans*, New International Commentary (Grand Rapids, MI: Eerdmans, 1996), 657; also Thomas Schreiner, *Romans*, Baker Exegetical Commentary on the New Testament (Grand Rapids, MI: Baker, 1998), 560.

Examine yourselves, to see whether you are in the faith. Test yourselves. Or do you not realize this about yourselves, that Jesus Christ is in you?—unless indeed you fail to meet the test!

This verse poses a challenge for Free Grace advocates because they do not think it appropriate to tell regular churchgoers who profess to be Christians that they should "examine themselves" to find out if they are really born again or not. That comes too close to saying that good works are a necessary result of saving faith, which is contrary to Free Grace teaching.

Therefore Hodges says that 2 Corinthians 13:5 is not a challenge to the churchgoers at Corinth to test whether they are, in fact, born-again Christians. It is rather a challenge to test whether they are "living in a dynamic, faith-oriented connection with Jesus Christ."[16] In other words, "Examine yourselves, to see whether you are in the faith" means to examine yourselves to see whether you are living a dynamic Christian life.[17]

Hodges supports this interpretation with reference to other verses about standing fast "in the faith" (1 Cor. 16:13) or being "sound in the faith" (Titus 1:13). But other verses that talk about the *condition* of one's life "in the faith" should not be equated with 2 Corinthians 13:5, where Paul is talking about whether they are "in the faith" *at all*. And Hodges completely fails to account for the fact that in the second half of the same verse, the test that Paul is seeking from them is further explained as finding out whether "Jesus Christ is in you," and Paul says

---

[16] Hodges, *Absolutely Free!*, 201.

[17] Similarly, Dillow says that in 2 Corinthians 13:5, "Salvation is not in view at all." Dillow, *Final Destiny*, 452.

Jesus is not in them if they "fail to meet the test." Surely the entire verse is talking about whether they are born-again Christian believers or not.

9. James 2:14–17

James writes,

> What good is it, my brothers, if someone says he has faith but does not have works? Can that faith save him? If a brother or sister is poorly clothed and lacking in daily food, and one of you says to them, 'Go in peace, be warmed and filled,' without giving them the things needed for the body, what good is that? So also faith by itself, if it does not have works, is dead.

These verses pose a significant challenge to the Free Grace position, because they seem to be saying that genuine faith will always result in good works. But, again, the Free Grace position argues that it is wrong to say that good works are a necessary result or a necessary evidence of saving faith.

Therefore Hodges has an alternative explanation. When James says, "Can that faith save him?" he is not talking about eternal salvation but about rescue from the destructive consequences of living a life of sin in this world. Hodges writes, "James is not talking here about salvation from hell. Why should he? He and his readers were born again" (and here Hodges mentions verses such as 1:2, 9, 16, 18; 2:1; 4:2–3 in which James assumes that his readers are saved). He continues, "James had no need whatsoever to discuss with his brethren the issue of salvation from hell." Hodges explains that James is therefore speaking about being "saved" "from the death-dealing consequences of sin" (that is, in this life) and "prolonging human life by godliness," something that "can only be effected by obedience—by good works."[18]

But Hodges fails to take into account the fact that James clearly signals that he is not talking about all his readers or even most of his readers but rather about "someone" with whom they are in contact. In the opening sentence of this section, James distinguishes this "someone" from the people to whom he is mostly writing, whom he calls "my brothers." He says, "What good is it, *my brothers*, if *someone* says he has faith but does not have works?" (James 2:14). Therefore when Hodges cites verses assuming that the general audience is made up of believers, he simply misses the point. James is talking about "someone" who may be in a different situation from most of the readers.[19]

In addition, Hodges fails to consider that whenever the Greek word *sōzō*—"save, deliver"—is used in the New Testament, it always refers to eternal salvation except where the context specifies

---

[18] Hodges, *Absolutely Free!*, 124–25. David Anderson says the verse means: "If a man has done no works for the glory of Christ, then none of the works of his life will be saved. He will be in heaven" (David R. Anderson, *Free Grace Soteriology*, ed. James Reitman, rev. ed. [The Woodlands, TX: Grace Theology Press, 2012], 19). However, the verse does not say, "Can that faith save *his works*," but, "Can that faith save *him*?" Other Free Grace authors adopt a similar interpretation. Charles Bing says the verse is talking about being "saved from having his unworthy works burned" or from "suffering a loss of reward" at the judgment seat of Christ (Bing, *Lordship Salvation*, 34). Joseph Dillow says that James 2:14, "Can that faith save him?" refers not to eternal salvation but to "salvation from loss at the judgment seat of Christ" (Dillow, *Final Destiny*, 402). Fred Chay and John Correia say that "the salvation in mind in 2:14–26 is the temporal deliverance from divine discipline of a believer" (Chay and Correia, *The Faith That Saves*, 136).

[19] The same oversight regarding the kind of person James is discussing in this verse characterizes the treatment of this passage by Fred Chay and John Correia. They argue that throughout the entire book James is addressing regenerate people, Christians. Then they say, regarding James 2:14, "If James shifts his address to unregenerate people in v. 14, he certainly does so without any marker and very abruptly." Chay and Correia, *The Faith That Saves*, 130. But they do not mention the crucial fact that in v. 14 James explicitly signals that he is talking not about "you" (most of his readers) but about "someone" (Greek *tis*).

a situation of rescue from physical danger or healing from physical sickness (as in James 5:15 or Matt. 8:25; 9:22, for example). But there is no such contextual specification in James 2:14–17. Therefore we are correct to understand it as referring to eternal salvation, which is consistent with its usage in every other New Testament context like this, where physical healing or physical rescue from danger is not specifically indicated.

This same consideration regarding the use of the Greek term *sōzō* also weighs heavily against Hodges's interpretation of another verse in James, which we will now consider.

10. James 2:26

James writes,

> For as the body apart from the spirit is dead, so also faith apart from works is dead.

See also James 2:17: "So also faith by itself, if it does not have works, is dead." Hodges says that in these verses the mention of "dead" faith shows that it was previously alive, and by this he implies that a person with such dead faith is still saved by virtue of his *previous* "living" faith. He writes, "In one of the strangest distortions of Scripture that has ever occurred, many theologians and Bible interpreters have decided that a 'dead faith' must necessarily have always been dead. But why draw such a deduction as this? James compares 'dead faith' to a dead body. . . . What James is worried about is a Christian whose faith has lost all of its vitality and productiveness."[20]

---

[20] Hodges, *Absolutely Free!*, 125–26. He notes that when we see a dead body, we naturally conclude that it was once alive. In many of Hodges's writings, one clue that he is about to lightly dismiss the widely accepted, plain meaning of a text is intemperate language of

But once again Hodges has failed to take adequate account of the context in which these verses occur. This entire section begins with the question that has to do with eternal salvation: "What good is it, my brothers, if someone says he has faith but does not have works? *Can that faith save him?*" (James 2:14). Because no physical danger or sickness is specified in the context, "save" here must be understood to refer to eternal salvation (as explained above). Therefore the entire passage (vv. 14–26) continues to deal with the topic of eternal salvation.

But the paragraph clearly implies that faith that "does not have works" *cannot save.* (The Greek word *mē* that introduces the question, "Can that faith save him?" is a word that shows the author is expecting the answer no to the question. It is as if the author wrote, "That faith cannot save him, can it?") Therefore James begins this entire paragraph by saying that faith without works cannot save someone.[21]

This means that Hodges is contradicting the entire force of the paragraph when he implies that a person with "dead faith" is still saved because that faith must have been alive at an earlier point.[22] James says nothing of the kind, nor does he imply that.

---

astonishment such as what he writes here: "In one of the strangest distortions of Scripture that has ever occurred . . ." We may categorize this style of argument as "dismissal by feigned astonishment."

[21] Tom Nettles quotes several statements from John Calvin's commentary on James 2:18–25 to show that Hodges has misquoted Calvin on this passage. Nettles says, "The rationale behind his quotes from Luther and Calvin is mystifying," and his quotations from Calvin are "from contexts which are arguments against principal parts of Hodges's whole scheme." He adds that several statements by Calvin on this passage show that, in direct opposition to the view of Hodges, "Calvin believed that 'works necessarily go along with faith' . . . [and] 'good works are invariably tied to faith.'" Nettles concludes, "Each of these statements directly contradicts clearly articulated statements of Hodges." Tom J. Nettles, "Review of Zane Clark Hodges, *Absolutely Free. A Biblical Reply to Lordship Salvation,*" *Trinity Journal* 11 (Fall 1990): 245–46.

[22] Similarly, Joseph Dillow says that "death is always preceded by life," so, "the dead faith to which James refers was unquestionably alive at one time, or it could not have died!" Dillow, *Final Destiny*, 418.

The only analogy he makes is with the *present* condition of the dead body, which can do nothing. Faith "without works" is exactly the kind that indicates that the person is not genuinely saved.

The analogy of a dead body is used only to show that a dead body can accomplish nothing, and this is parallel to someone who *claims* to have spiritual life ("faith") but does not really have any, just like a body without a spirit. (The argument that when we see a dead human body, we realize that it was once alive does not apply here, any more than it would apply to Ephesians 2:1–2, where Paul says, "You were dead in the trespasses and sins in which you once walked." He does not imply that they were previously spiritually alive, for they had always been spiritually dead.)

This means that James says that a person with dead faith, faith without works that follow, is not saved. Such faith cannot "save him" (v. 14). But Hodges says that such a person is saved. And that means that in Hodges's view, but contrary to the consistent testimony of Scripture, unbelievers go to heaven.[23]

11. James 5:19–20

Later in James we read,

> My brothers, if anyone among you wanders from the truth and someone brings him back, let him know that whoever brings back a sinner from his wandering *will save his soul from death* and will cover a multitude of sins.

---

[23] I am indebted to Dan Wallace for this observation. He, in turn, attributes it to our mutual friend Sam Storms.

The Free Grace position does not want to admit that a "sinner" who wanders away from Christian fellowship is in danger of eternal death, as this passage seems to imply. Therefore Hodges claims that "save his soul from death" means rescuing a Christian from a premature physical death that would come through God's discipline: "Apart from repentance the sinning Christian is headed toward an untimely death under the chastening hand of God."[24]

But no physical danger or physical sickness or other threat to physical life is specified by this context, and, therefore, consistent with New Testament usage of this verb elsewhere, it is far better to understand this as referring to eternal salvation. And that means that this verse also argues against the Free Grace position, for it assumes that there are people "among you" (that is, in the church) who are professing Christians but are in danger of eternal condemnation, as shown by their sinful pattern of life. James urges his readers to care for such a person and try to bring him back from his "wandering," for this "will save his soul from death."

This pattern of idiosyncratic, eccentric interpretations, as illustrated in the verses above, continues nearly everywhere one looks in Free Grace literature. We are told that some Christians "receive" eternal life but do not "possess" it,[25] that some Christians will be "in" the kingdom of heaven but they will not "inherit it,"[26] that Christ will present only some Christians, not all, as "holy and blameless and above reproach before him"

---

24 Hodges, *Absolutely Free!*, 160.
25 Anderson, *Free Grace Soteriology*, 138.
26 Dillow, *Final Destiny*, 56, 89–90.

(Col. 1:22),[27] that some Christians will be able to enter the heavenly city but will not "enter by the gates,"[28] and that some Christians will be "cast out" from the marriage supper of the Lamb in heaven and will experience "weeping and gnashing of teeth" (Matt. 22:13), even though they are still saved.[29]

Every verse in the New Testament that challenges the Free Grace view is made into a new, special category, so that it applies only to a select group of believers, not all. Then Free Grace supporters can say that people who are not in that special category are still saved. And all of this is done by seminary graduates who have the ability to use technical tools such as concordances and reference books for New Testament Greek, giving their writings the appearance of scholarly argument. But it is technical argument that lacks sound judgment and cannot stand up under careful scrutiny by evangelical scholars outside the Free Grace movement.[30]

It is not surprising that Thomas Schreiner expresses some measure of amazement and even frustration at dealing with such Free Grace arguments (in this case, the arguments of Robert Wilkin, executive director of the Grace Evangelical Society,

---

[27] Ibid., 365–66.

[28] Ibid., 939.

[29] Ibid., 770–78. Not all Free Grace supporters hold this view, but Dillow's book was still the first book offered for sale in July 2015 on the website of the Free Grace Alliance, which suggests that the organization holds Dillow's book in high esteem.

[30] That is probably the reason why nearly all Free Grace publications are published by their own organizations or are self-published by the individual authors. With the exception of the book by Zane Hodges, *Absolutely Free!*, which was published by Zondervan as an alternative viewpoint to the simultaneous publication of John MacArthur's *The Gospel According to Jesus: What Is Authentic Faith?*, anniversary ed. (Grand Rapids, MI: Zondervan, 2008), and a 2009 Kregel book by Charles Bing that is now out of print, I am not aware of any Free Grace book that has been published by a recognized, mainstream evangelical, academic publisher (such as Zondervan, Baker, Crossway, InterVarsity Press, P&R, B&H, or others). This means that (with two exceptions) their publications have not made it through the rigorous editorial vetting process that established publishers undertake before they will publish a manuscript.

but his comments are generally applicable to what I see in Free Grace interpretations again and again):

> What could ever convince Wilkin and those who support him that they are wrong? If the text says good works are necessary for eternal life [and here Schreiner is discussing Galatians 6:7–9, where Paul says that "the one who sows to the Spirit will from the Spirit reap eternal life"], then (according to Wilkin) the eternal life is different from the eternal life that brings salvation. . . . No evidence could ever be adduced that would prove the contrary. For even if the Bible were to say, "good works are necessary for eternal life and to escape hell," it seems that Wilkin would say, "eternal life and hell have a different meaning here."[31]

It is not surprising that D. A. Carson writes about Zane Hodges, "To the best of my knowledge not one significant interpreter of Scripture in the entire history of the church has held to Hodges' pattern of interpretation of the passages he treats," and he says that Hodges's approach results in "many, many utterly novel (and, I fear, unconvincing) exegeses."[32]

Regarding Zane Hodges's view of the gospel, Michael Horton writes,

> As James Boice, J. I. Packer, and others have argued in their works, no respected, mainstream Christian thinker,

---

[31] Thomas Schreiner, "Response to Robert N. Wilkin," in *The Role of Works at the Final Judgment*, ed. Alan Stanley (Grand Rapids, MI: Zondervan, 2013), 55. Schreiner is not arguing that good works are necessary for justification but rather that "the faith that saves is never alone" because it is always accompanied by good works, and numerous New Testament passages such as Galatians 6:7–9 point to that conclusion.

[32] D. A. Carson, *Exegetical Fallacies*, 2nd ed. (Grand Rapids, MI: Baker, 1996), 129. Carson is referring specifically to Hodges's *The Gospel under Siege* (Dallas: Redencion Viva, 1981).

writer, or preacher has ever held such extreme and unusual views concerning the nature of the gospel and saving grace as Zane Hodges.[33]

Yet Hodges's teachings and writings have been the primary driving force behind the resurgence of the modern Free Grace movement for several decades.

---

[33] Michael Horton, *Christ the Lord: The Reformation and Lordship Salvation* (Eugene, OR: Wipf and Stock, 1992), 11.

Conclusion

A. Summary of the argument of this book

In the preceding chapters I have attempted to demonstrate that the New Testament clearly and repeatedly teaches the following two points, which differ with the heart of the Free Grace Gospel:

> 1) *Repentance from sin* (in the sense of remorse for sin and an internal resolve to forsake it) is necessary for saving faith,

and

> 2) *Good works* and *continuing to believe* necessarily follow from saving faith.

In addition, I argued that these two points are entirely consistent with the great Reformation teaching that "we are justified by faith alone, but the faith that justifies is never alone." I further argued that the mistakes of the Free Grace movement today all stem from a misunderstanding of the way the word *alone* is used in the expression "justification by faith alone."

My concerns were organized into five chapters, covering one historical concern and four practical concerns, as follows.

Chapter 1. The Free Grace movement does not teach the

Reformation doctrine of justification by faith alone, because it holds a historically unusual view that is based on a misunderstanding of *alone* in the historic Protestant insistence on "justification by faith alone."

Chapter 2. The Free Grace movement weakens the gospel message by avoiding any call to unbelievers to repent of their sins. The result is that some followers of Free Grace teaching have never repented of their sins, and they are not saved.

Chapter 3. The Free Grace movement gives false assurance of eternal life to many people who profess faith in Christ but then show no evidence in their pattern of life or even in continuing to say that they believe in Christ. The result is that many people have been assured that they are saved, but they are not.

Chapter 4. The Free Grace movement leads its supporters to overemphasize one necessary component of genuine faith (mental assent to the Bible's propositions about Christ's atoning work) and to underemphasize another necessary component of genuine faith (namely, heartfelt trust in the living person of Jesus Christ as my Savior and my God). The result is that some followers of the Free Grace movement intellectually agree with the right doctrines, but they have never trusted in Christ as a person, and they are not truly saved.

Chapter 5. The Free Grace movement promotes numerous highly unusual, highly unlikely interpretations of the New Testament because of their need to defend a mistaken understanding of the word *alone* in the phrase "faith alone."

Because of these concerns, I cannot recommend Free Grace teachings, or the Free Grace movement, as a legitimate option for evangelicals to accept and follow.

B. Topics not covered in this book

As I explained at the beginning of the book (p. 22–24), I decided not to treat the question of "lordship salvation" in this book, because I concluded that framing the question in terms of Christ's lordship would not adequately focus the main differences between the Free Grace movement and the rest of evangelical Protestantism. For a similar reason, I decided not to treat some other topics related to this discussion.

I did not discuss the question of whether there are different kinds of faith mentioned in the New Testament (such as saving faith and various kinds of nonsaving faith), because the key differences with the Free Grace movement regarding faith are rather (1) whether trust in the person of Christ and not just trust in facts about him is necessary for saving faith, and (2) whether people can have assurance that their faith is real when there is no evident fruit of that faith in their lives.

I also did not discuss the question of whether there is such a thing as a "carnal Christian." That is because people on both sides of the debate would admit that sometimes a genuine believer can experience an extended time of backsliding and give little if any evidence of saving faith. The question is not whether that can happen. The question is whether we should give assurance of eternal salvation to a person who once understood the gospel clearly and made a believable profession of faith but now claims to have no faith in Christ and shows no evidence of regeneration in his or her life. According to the Free Grace view, such a person is still saved and should be given assurance of salvation. But according to the historic

Protestant view, we have no basis for giving assurance of salvation.

In addition, I did not get into any differences between Reformed and Arminian Christians regarding salvation, because the Free Grace position differs not only with Reformed evangelical theology but also with all of evangelical Arminian theology since the Reformation.

C. What do I appreciate about the Free Grace movement?

As is evident in the previous pages, I cannot say that I appreciate any of the doctrinal distinctives of the Free Grace movement that set it apart from historic Protestantism. And I think that those distinctives have had, for the most part, a harmful influence upon evangelicals around the world.

However, as I mentioned at the beginning of the book, I am thankful for the friendships and the exemplary Christian lives and ministries of numerous Free Grace supporters whom I have known. Many of them have, in spite of this distinctive teaching, developed very significant, kingdom-advancing ministries around the world.

I also believe that this entire controversy has served to give a strong warning to contemporary evangelicals that we must always zealously guard the great Reformation truth of justification by faith alone. We must never begin to teach that justification comes by faith plus works, even a little bit of works. While we must insist on repentance, we must never slip into teaching that a little "cleaning up" of one's life is necessary before repentance is genuine!

The Free Grace movement has also reminded us so clearly

that born-again Christians can and should be able to have assurance of eternal life and that this is one of the great blessings offered to us in the New Testament.

Finally, I believe that one very positive benefit that could come from this controversy is a healthy reexamining of our beliefs and practices throughout the whole evangelical world regarding repentance, the nature of saving faith, and assurance of salvation.

D. My hope for the future

I sincerely hope that many Free Grace supporters, while perhaps finding this book hard to read, will also be able to seriously consider it as an attempt at a kind of "family intervention" by a brother who loves them very much and is earnestly pleading with them to change their viewpoint. I hope they will see that the Free Grace view is inconsistent with the Bible and come to agree that justification by faith alone does not require that faith *is* alone in the person who believes; that genuine repentance from sin is a necessary part of saving faith; and that genuine faith, according to the New Testament, will always result in evident good works and in a faith that continues until the end of our lives.

I also hope that evangelicals who read this book and do not hold to Free Grace positions will be challenged in their evangelism never to avoid or water down the frequent New Testament calls to unbelievers to sincerely repent of their sins as they come to seek forgiveness in Christ (even though we live in a culture that will mock such preaching as harsh and judgmental). I also hope that in their evangelism they will emphasize the need not only for non-Christians to believe that the teachings of the Bible are true but also for a clear decision of their will to trust in Christ as a person in whose very presence they live and move and have their being. And I hope that evangelical pastors and other leaders will be challenged to refrain from giving unqualified assurance of salvation to those who were once part of an evangelical church but who now give no evidence of a living faith in Christ or of the kind of good works that will always follow from genuine faith.

Finally, I earnestly hope that after reading this book, any Free Grace followers who have never truly repented of their sins, who have never seen any evident change in their lives, and who have never sincerely received Christ and believed in him as a person will decide to turn from their sin, trust in Christ as a living person, and, for the first time, be truly born again. "Therefore, if anyone is in Christ, he is a new creation. The old has passed away; behold, the new has come" (2 Cor. 5:17).

Bibliography

Allison, Gregg. *Historical Theology*. Grand Rapids, MI: Zondervan, 2011.

"Assemblies of God Statement of Fundamental Truths." June 23, 2015. http://agchurches.org/Sitefiles/Default/RSS/AG.org%20TOP/Beliefs/SFT_2011.pdf.

Anderson, David R. *Free Grace Soteriology*. Edited by James Reitman. The Woodlands, TX: Grace Theology Press, 2012.

Berkhof, Louis. *Systematic Theology*. Grand Rapids, MI: Eerdmans, 1941.

Bing, Charles. *Grace, Salvation, and Discipleship: How to Understand Some Difficult Bible Passages*. The Woodlands, TX: Grace Theology Press, 2015.

———. *Lordship Salvation: A Biblical Evaluation and Response*. Maitland, FL: Xulon Press, 2010.

Bond, J. B., Gary Derickson, Brad Doskocil, et al. *The Grace New Testament Commentary*. 2 vols. Denton, TX: Grace Evangelical Society, 2010.

Brown, Michael L. *Hyper-Grace: Exposing the Dangers of the Modern Grace Message*. Lake Mary, FL: Charisma House, 2014.

Calvin, John. *Institutes of the Christian Religion*. 2 vols. Translated by Ford Lewis Battles.
Philadelphia: Westminster, 1960.

———. "John Calvin Tracts and Letters—Acts of the Council of Trent," February 15,
2014. http://www.godrules.net/library/calvin/142calvin_c4.htm.

Carson, D. A. *Exegetical Fallacies*. Grand Rapids, MI: Baker, 1996.

Catechism of the Catholic Church. New York: Doubleday, 1997.

Chay, Fred, and John Correia. *The Faith That Saves*. Dallas, TX: Grace Line, 2008.

Clark, Gordon Haddon. *What Is Saving Faith?* Unicoi, TN: Trinity Foundation, 2004.

Clark, R. E. D. "Sandemanians." In *New International Dictionary of the Christian Church*, edited by J. D. Douglas. Grand Rapids, MI: Zondervan, 1974, 877.

Dillow, Joseph. *Final Destiny: The Future Reign of the Servant Kings*. Monument, CO: Paniym Group, 2012.

———. *The Reign of the Servant Kings: A Study of Eternal Security and the Final Destiny of Man*. 2nd ed. Monument, CO: Paniym Group, 2012.

Erickson, Millard. *Christian Theology*. Grand Rapids, MI: Baker, 1998.

Frame, John. *Systematic Theology*. Phillipsburg, NJ: P&R, 2013.

Free Grace Alliance. "Covenant." January 19, 2015. http://www.freegracealliance.com/covenant.htm.

Gentry, Kenneth. "The Great Option: A Study of the Lordship Controversy." *Baptist Reformation Review*, no. 5 (Spring, 1976).

———. *Lord of the Saved: Getting to the Heart of the Lordship Debate*. Phillipsburg, NJ: P&R, 1992. Reprinted Fountain Inn, SC: Victorious House, 2001.

"Glasites (also Sandemanians)." In *The Oxford Dictionary of the Christian Church*, edited by F. L. Cross. Oxford, UK: Oxford University Press, 1974.

Gower, Ralph. *The New Manners and Customs of Bible Times*. Chicago: Moody Press, 1987.

Grace Evangelical Society. "Affirmations of Belief," February 6, 2015. http://www.faith-alone.org/about/beliefs.html.

Grudem, Wayne. *Systematic Theology*. Grand Rapids, MI: Zondervan, 2010.

Guthrie, Donald. *New Testament Introduction*. Downers Grove, IL: InterVarsity Press, 1970.

Harrison, Everett, and John Stott. "Must Christ Be Lord to Be Savior? No . . . Yes." *Eternity* 10.9, September 1959, 13–18, 36, 48.

Hixson, J. B., Rick Whitmire, and Roy B. Zuck., eds. *Freely by His Grace: Classical Free Grace Theology*. Duluth, MN: Grace Gospel Press, 2012.

Hodge, Charles. *Systematic Theology*. 3 vols. Grand Rapids, MI: Eerdmans, 1970.

Hodges, Zane. *Absolutely Free! A Biblical Reply to Lordship Salvation*. Grand Rapids, MI: Zondervan, 1989.

———. *A Free Grace Primer*. Corinth, TX: Grace Evangelical Society, 2011.

———. *Grace in Eclipse: A Study on Eternal Rewards*. 2nd edition. Dallas: Redencion Viva, 1987.

———. *Harmony with God: A Fresh Look at Repentance*. Dallas: Redención Viva, 2001.

Horton, Michael, ed. *Christ the Lord: The Reformation and Lordship Salvation*. Eugene, OR: Wipf & Stock, 2008.

Knight, George W., III. *The Pastoral Epistles: A Commentary on the Greek Text*. New International Greek Testament Commentary. Grand Rapids, MI: Eerdmans, 1992.

Lybrand, Fred R. *Back to Faith: Reclaiming Gospel Clarity in an Age of Incongruence*. Camarillo, CA: Xulon Press, 2009.

MacArthur, John F., Jr. *Faith Works: The Gospel According to the Apostles*. Dallas: Word, 1993.

———. *The Gospel According to Jesus: What Is Authentic Faith?* Anniversary edition. Grand Rapids, MI: Zondervan, 2008.

———. "Repentance in the Gospel of John." *Grace to You* website. March 28, 2015. http://www.gty.org-/resources/print/articles/A238.

Machen, J. Gresham. *What Is Faith?* Grand Rapids, MI: Eerdmans, 1969.

McKinley, Mike. *Am I Really a Christian?* Wheaton, IL: Crossway, 2011.

Moo, Douglas. *The Epistle to the Romans*. New International Commentary. Grand Rapids, MI: Eerdmans, 1996.

Morris, Leon. *The Epistle to the Romans*. Pillar New Testament Commentary. Grand Rapids, MI: Eerdmans, 1988.

Moulton, James, and George Milligan. *The Vocabulary of the Greek New Testament: Illustrated from the Papyri and Other Non-Literary Sources*. Grand Rapids, MI: Eerdmans, 1930.

Muller, Richard A. *Post-Reformation Reformed Dogmatics*. 2nd edition. 4 vols. Grand Rapids, MI: Baker, 2003.

Nettles, Tom. J. "Review of Zane Clark Hodges, Absolutely Free: A Biblical Reply to Lordship Salvation." *Trinity Journal* 11 (Fall 1990): 242–47.

Peterson, Robert A. *Our Secure Salvation: Preservation and Apostasy*. Phillipsburg, NJ: P&R, 2009.

Pliny, *Natural History*. Translated by H. Rackham. Loeb Classical Library. Cambridge, MA: Harvard University Press, 1950.

Robertson, Archibald T. *Word Pictures in the New Testament*. 6 vols. Grand Rapids, MI: Baker, 1931.

Schaff, Philip, ed. *The Creeds of Christendom*. 3 vols. Grand Rapids, MI: Baker, 1983.

Schreiner, Thomas. *Romans*. Baker Exegetical Commentary on the New Testament. Grand Rapids, MI: Baker, 1998.

———. "Response to Robert N. Wilkin." In *The Role of Works at the Final Judgment*. Edited by Alan Stanley. Grand Rapids, MI: Zondervan, 2013.

Schultz, A. C. "Vine, vineyard." In *Zondervan Pictorial Encyclopedia of the Bible*. Edited by Merrill Tenney. Grand Rapids, MI: Zondervan, 1975.

Silva, Moises, ed. *New International Dictionary of New Testament Theology and Exegesis*.

5 vols. Grand Rapids, MI: Zondervan, 2014.

Wallace, Daniel. *Greek Grammar beyond the Basics*. Grand Rapids, MI: Zondervan, 1996.

Walsh, Carey. *The Fruit of the Vine: Viticulture in Ancient Israel.* Winona Lake, IN: Eisenbrauns, 2000.

Warfield, B. B. "The Biblical Doctrine of Faith." In *Biblical Doctrines*, vol. 2 of *The Works of Benjamin B. Warfield.* Grand Rapids, MI: Baker, 1991.

———. "On Faith in Its Psychological Aspects." In *Studies in Theology*, vol. 9, *The Works of Benjamin B. Warfield.* Grand Rapids, MI: Baker, 1991.

Wesley, John. "The Law Established Through Faith." Sermon 35, 1872. http://wesley.-nnu.edu/john-wesley/the-sermons-of-john -wesley-1872-edition/sermon-35-thelaw-established-through -faith-discourse-one/.

Wilkin, Robert N. *The Ten Most Misunderstood Words in the Bible.* Corinth, TX: Grace Evangelical Society, 2012.

———. "What Is Free Grace Theology?" *Grace in Focus* 29.5, September/October 2014, 27.

Wilkin, Robert N., Thomas R. Schreiner, James D. G. Dunn, Michael P. Barber, and Stanley N. Gundry. *Four Views on the Role of Works at the Final Judgment.* Edited by Alan P. Stanley. Grand Rapids, MI: Zondervan, 2013.

General Index

Scripture Index

Also Available from Wayne Grudem

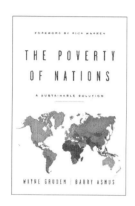

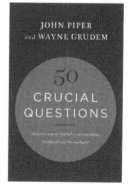

For more information, visit crossway.org.

Made in the USA
Charleston, SC
16 September 2016